ABUNDANT

Life More ABUNDANT

Spirit-Filled Messages From the Keswick Convention

W. GRAHAM SCROGGIE • ANDREW MURRAY
R. A. TORREY • EVAN H. HOPKINS
CHARLES INNWOOD • PAUL S. REES
J. H. LINTON • J. STUART HOLDEN
ALAN REDPATH

Edited by **HERBERT F. STEVENSON**

FRANCIS ASBURY PRESS
of Zondervan Publishing House

Grand Rapids. Michigan

LIFE MORE ABUNDANT
Copyright © 1987 by Marshall-Pickering
3 Beggarwood Lane,
Basingstoke, Hants RG23 7LP England

Extracts taken from:
Keswick's Authentic Voice, ed. Herbert F. Stevenson
Copyright © 1959 Marshall, Morgan and Scott

Keswick's Triumphant Voice, ed. Herbert F. Stevenson
Copyright © 1963 Marshall, Morgan and Scott

FRANCIS ASBURY PRESS is an imprint of
Zondervan Publishing House
1415 Lake Drive, S.E.
Grand Rapids, Michigan 49506

Library of Congress Cataloging in Publication Data
Keswick Convention.
    Life more abundant.

    Sermons, English. 2. Keswick movement. I. Stevenson, Herbert F.
II. Title.
BV4241.K45 1987   252   87-10420
ISBN 0-310-20071-7

Printed in the United States of America

87 88 89 90 91 92 93 / CH / 9 8 7 6 5 4 3 2 1

CONTENTS

FOREWORD:
Keswick and Its Message

Most religious movements have roots reaching back into an era before their actual inception. So it is with the Keswick Convention. Long before the first gatherings in a tent erected in a field adjoining the grounds of St. John's Vicarage, Keswick, in 1875 (which proved to be the initiation of the annual Keswick assembly), the teachings concerning the "deepening of the spiritual life" now associated with the name of Keswick had long been exemplified in the lives of Christian people of many races and generations, set forth in books in various languages.

But the most amazing phenomenon of church history is the way in which vital doctrines become forgotten and temporarily lost. So it was with the central truth of the Christian faith, which was obscured and buried under the trappings of Rome until Martin Luther rediscovered it in the glorious phrase, "justified by faith." Likewise the Scripture's clear presentation of the "life more abundant" in Christ was strangely neglected from medieval times until the middle of the nineteenth century. Yet Luther himself had gone on from justification by faith to "the fullness of the blessing of the gospel of Christ." And in England a book published near the end of the seventeenth century by the Puritan divine Walter Marshall contained all that Keswick later reminted in present-day language.

It is amazing that this obscure Fellow of Winchester College should have come through personal study of the Scriptures to so clear an understanding of an aspect of the truth that was generally disregarded. His book had a cumbersome title, characteristic of those days: *The Gospel Mystery of Sanctification, Opened in Sundry Practical Directions Suited Especially to Cases of those who Labour under the Guilt and Power of Indwelling Sin.* This is customarily abbreviated to its first phrase, *The Gospel Mystery of Sanctification.* Remarkable as Marshall's book is, its author had no idea that he was proclaiming anything new; his purpose was to present, simply and clearly, what the Scriptures say on the subject of sanctification. And his book ran through several editions.

There was accordingly nothing original about this message when it was declared again at the Keswick Convention; yet it came with a freshness and vitality that virtually amounted to a new revelation to a generation that had long neglected this glorious divine provision for holy living.

Keswick was an indirect result of the 1859 Revival, which lifted the entire tone of life in both America and Great Britain, and which set in motion dynamic forces of social reform that are with us still. One of the most notable effects of the revival was to awaken a sense of spiritual poverty and powerlessness in the hearts and minds of people who in ordinary times would have been regarded as outstanding in saintliness and spiritual fervor. Such a consciousness could not be ignored or suppressed—unlike the way in which such an awareness is too easily ignored today. Christians' quest for victory over every known besetting sin and for fullness of power in Christian service led them to reexamine the scriptural teaching concerning holiness. And God, who awakened their sense of need, provided the answer.

It was in America that the rediscovery was made. Dr. W. E. Boardman gave it early expression in his famous book, *The Higher Christian Life,* which made a deep impression and met a widely felt need. In this book he recounted the experiences and teaching of Luther, Merle D'Aubigne (the historian of the Reformation), and many others, including John Wesley. The teaching was eagerly welcomed and widely disseminated at meetings convened for this purpose and through dozens of books. Among its most gifted exponents were Mr. and Mrs. Robert Pearsall Smith, a Quaker couple who had "come into the blessing" and later joined the Presbyterian Church. They became missionaries of the higher-life message to Europe. Not only were they both eloquent speakers, but Mrs. Pearsall Smith (Hannah Whitall Smith) was also an able writer, and her book entitled *The Christian's Secret of a Happy Life* is still a classic of Keswick teaching.

They addressed a number of gatherings in England in 1873. One meeting small in attendance but significant in its outcome was held at Curzon Chapel, London. Among the sixteen or so persons present were two destined to take a leading part in future conventions at Keswick, Evan H. Hopkins and E. W. Moore. Mrs. Hopkins tells how, on returning home, her husband was "like one looking out on a wide land and beautiful, flowing with milk and honey. He knew that it was to be possessed, and that *it was his.*" Mr. Moore wrote long afterwards that "from that little meeting, as from an obscure source and spring, the stream of Keswick teaching and influence, which has gone round the world since then, may truly be said to have taken its rise."

In the following year, a six-day conference was held at Broadlands near Romsey, Hants, the country seat of the Rt. Hon.

W. Cowper-Temple, a minister of Parliament. Among the hundred guests at that conference were eminent people from all walks of life. So deep an impression was made by the addresses given that many entered into a richer spiritual experience than ever before, transforming their lives and ministries.

Among them was a visitor from the Continent, Pasteur Theodore Monod, who during that memorable week wrote his moving hymn, "Oh, the Bitter Shame and Sorrow."

Those attending the Broadlands conference soon arranged a larger conference at Oxford for August 29 to September 7, 1874. A large company gathered, including a number of Evangelical leaders from the Continent. A great blessing was experienced here as at Broadlands. "God hath visited His people!" a contemporary report declared. "God has opened the windows of heaven and is pouring out a blessing that there shall not be room to receive it!" It was indeed akin to revival, not in convicting and converting the unsaved, but in bringing the children of God into "life more abundant."

One of these was Canon T. D. Harford-Battersby, vicar of St. John's, Keswick, a devout man who was yet unsatisfied with his own spiritual life. While the Rev. Evan Hopkins was speaking on the healing of the nobleman's son (John 4:46ff.) and describing the difference between a seeking and a resting faith, the Canon said to himself, I WILL *rest in Him*. Later he testified, "I got a revelation of Christ to my soul, so extraordinary, glorious and precious, that from that day it illuminated my life. I found *He* was *all* I wanted. I shall never forget it; the day and hour are present with me. How it humbled me, and yet what peace it brought!"

A still larger convention was held at Brighton in the early summer of 1875, when remarkable scenes were witnessed. That gathering is scarcely in the genealogy of Keswick, although it was one of its most notable forerunners. During it, Canon Harford-Battersby and a prominent Quaker, Mr. Robert Wilson, arranged for a series of "union meetings for the promotion of practical holiness" to be held at Keswick from July 29, 1875, at which Mr. and Mrs. Pearsall Smith were to be the principal speakers. A breakdown on the part of Mr. Smith not only prevented his keeping this engagement but obliged him to retire from public ministry. Nothing daunted, the conveners secured other speakers for the meeting at Keswick, notably the Rev. W. H. Webb-Peploe, who from that first year became a dominating figure on the Keswick platform.

With the withdrawal of the American couple who had been so signally used of God in conferences held throughout England, the movement became focused in the Keswick Convention, which grew steadily from year to year in numbers and influence. Canon Harford-Battersby presided until his death in 1883; but perhaps the outstanding personality, both on the platform and behind the scenes, was the Rev. Evan H. Hopkins. The "theologian of Keswick," Mr. Hopkins more than any other man defined its distinctive message. He was a most gifted speaker and became editor of *The Christian's Pathway of Power*, a monthly paper begun by Mr. Pearsall Smith in 1874. Mr. Hopkins had contributed to the very first issue and soon assumed full responsibility for it.

The Christian's Pathway of Power naturally became closely linked with the Keswick Convention; and as its editor, Mr. Hopkins made it a powerful medium of Keswick teaching. In 1879 the name of the paper was changed to *The Life of Faith*, and in 1892 it became a weekly instead of a monthly. Its early volumes are the primary source of information concerning the convention in its formative years.

There was a spontaneity about the early conventions that imparted a remarkable vitality to the gatherings. No program was prearranged, but the conveners and speakers waited upon the leading of the Spirit of God from day to day. All of the addresses were extemporaneous. Those taking part had all experienced the liberating power of the message they proclaimed, and they spoke out of glowing hearts.

Spontaneity was never allowed to degenerate into diffusiveness, however; the convention had a clear purpose and kept strictly to it. Without deliberate premeditation, a progression of teaching soon took shape—beginning with the exceeding sinfulness of sin (especially sin in the believer), consequent defeat and power-lessness in life and witness, and God's provision for rehabilitation of the sinner in Christ. This sequence of teaching has never been followed in a mechanical way at Keswick; it is simply the underlying pattern, Spirit-given and developed year by year in the liberty of the Spirit.

Through the years, successive generations of speakers have been raised up to maintain the testimony of Keswick and to proclaim its message. Perhaps the "fire in the bones" of the early speakers has not been so evident in some of later years; but thousands still attend the Keswick Convention annually, hungering and thirsting for God until they find the answer to their need. In the addresses that follow, we have the full range of Keswick teaching as given by its most renowned exponents. Here we have indeed the authentic message of Keswick.

Herbert F. Stevenson
Keswick, England

ABOUNDING LIFE

W. GRAHAM SCROGGIE was a distinguished British Baptist minister who served as pastor of several congregations in Scotland and England, including the Spurgeon Tabernacle in London (1938–44). He spoke at Keswick meetings from 1912 until 1954.

ABOUNDING LIFE

Rev. W. Graham Scroggie, D.D.

I am come that they might have life, and that they might have it more abundantly—John 10: 10.

On Monday, July 28, 1875, there was inaugurated in this place what is now universally known as the Keswick Convention. During this period the number of persons who have attended these annual gatherings cannot, in the aggregate, have been less than 200,000. These have been drawn from every part of the world, and have been representative of every Protestant denomination.

All who have attended Keswick will know what it stands for, but there are numberless people besides who think of the convention in various ways: some with mere curiosity, some with a noncommittal interest, and some more critically. And so it may be well, at this the commencement of another season of holy convocation, to recall and reaffirm what has been the distinctive message of Keswick throughout these years, and what immediately we are here for, ever remembering that a movement must be judged by what it professes and undertakes to do, and not by what lies outside its scope.

Of course there are some things that are taken for granted: things which, though not our distinctive message, are the foundation and warrant of it: such truths, for instance, as the evangelical doctrines of the Person and work of Christ, His real humanity, His proper Deity, and His atoning sacrifice on Calvary. Also the need and adequacy of the Gospel in this world of sin; and, as being our first source of knowledge of these things, the veracity and authority of the Scriptures of the Old and New Testaments. These truths are not Keswick's distinctive teaching, for they are held and taught by all branches of Evangelical Christendom; but here they are assumed.

What, then, it may be asked, is the distinctive message of this movement? A former distinguished leader was once asked what was the difference between a conference and a convention, and after a moment's reflection he replied, "A conference has a subject, but a convention has an object." As applied to Keswick, that is not a mere epigram, but a great truth. This convention has an object, and that object is nowhere so briefly and adequately expressed as in the words of our text, "I am come that they might have life, and that they might have it more abundantly." Here Christ distinguishes between "life" and "life more abundant," and it is for the interpretation of this distinction, and that we might know experimentally this maximum life, that we are now gathered.

> 'Tis life, not death, for which we pant;
> More life, and fuller, that we want.

We cannot but have been impressed in our reading of the New Testament, especially of the writings of Paul and John, with the high level on which their thought moves when dealing with the subject of the Christian life. Phrase after phrase stands out in mystic grandeur of truths which have their origin in heaven, and their home in the human heart: such passages, for example, as, "For me to live is Christ"; "I count all things but loss for the excellency of the knowledge of Christ Jesus my Lord"; "I am crucified with Christ: nevertheless I live: yet not I, but Christ liveth in me: and the life which I now live in the flesh, I live by the faith of the Son of God, who loved me and gave Himself for me." And accompanying such passages as these, are others which point the way to the realisation of the blessed secret, such as, "Let us go on unto perfection"; "Being confident of this very thing, that He who hath begun a good work in you will perform it until the day of Jesus Christ"; "Be filled with the Spirit"; "Know the love of Christ, which passeth knowledge, that ye might be filled unto all the fulness of God"; "Having therefore these promises, dearly beloved, let us cleanse ourselves from all filthiness of the flesh and spirit, perfecting holiness in the fear of God." And there are yet other Scriptures which show the need of these, and which illustrate the fact that one may have life, and yet not have abounding life; that one may have the assurance of spiritual union with Christ, and yet be a stranger, for the most part, to that communion which is alone the outcome of obedience and trust.

Two illustrations will suffice. Remonstrating with the fickle Galatians, Paul says, "Are ye so foolish? Having begun in the Spirit, are ye now made perfect by the flesh?" Better-instructed Christians than they were are making the same mistake; and the matter is of vital importance, for we can never rise to the level of experience set forth in the foregoing texts so long as we are providing substitutes for the Holy Spirit.

But perhaps the immediate point is best illustrated by the

words of Peter at the time of his vision at Joppa. He saw, as it were, a great sheet let down from heaven, full of creatures clean and unclean, and when bidden to rise, slay, and eat, he replied, "Not so, Lord." How glaring a contradiction stands fixed in those words! He who says, "Not so," should never add "Lord," and he who truly says "Lord" never will say "Not so."

From these, and such-like passages of Holy Scripture, we must sadly acknowledge that Christians in general have been, and are, content with an experience far removed from the divine ideal. We have made the intellectual apprehension of truth a substitute for the power of it in our hearts, and are in danger of regarding Christianity as a philosophy rather than as a life. Christ is the complete answer alike to every false ground of hope, and every false theory of life. The answer to legalism is "Christ died for us," and the answer to licence is, "We must die with Christ." Religious belief is not enough: there must be moral change. It is the discrepancy between our profession and our experience that needs looking to; and we must deal with it, not in the twilight of past attainment, but in the noontide of divine possibility. The Christ, who dying did a work for us, now lives to do a work in us. "I am come that they might have life, and that they might have it more abundantly." There is great need that the truth be broadcast that abounding life is possible; and it should encourage us to know that in the experience of a multitude it has been, and is, actual.

All Christians have what the New Testament calls "eternal life," for without this one cannot be a Christian; but not all Christians have entered into the experience of abounding life. There can be relationship without fellowship; there can be union without communion; there can be life without health; there can be privilege without enjoyment; there can be movement without progress. One may war and yet not win, may serve and yet not succeed, may try and yet not triumph; and the difference throughout is just the difference between the possession of eternal life, and the experience of abounding life; the difference between "peace with God" and "the peace of God"; the difference between obtainment and attainment. Abounding life is just the fulness of life in Christ, made possible by His death and resurrection, and made actual by the indwelling and infilling of the Holy Spirit. It is not the will of God that we should be as fruitless trees, as waterless clouds, or as savourless salt; but that we should fulfil the highest functions of our Christian calling. Christ's promise is that He will slake the thirst of all who come to Him, and His purpose for those who come is that "out of their vitals shall flow rivers of living water."

The trouble and tragedy is that the Church has been content to live between Easter and Pentecost; on the right side of justification, but on the wrong side of sanctification; on the right side of pardon, but on the wrong side of power. The difference between the world and the Church is in the relation of each to Calvary. But it is not enough that the Church and the Christian be on the right side of Easter, which has brought us forgiveness and life; we are called also to the experience of Pentecost, which offers to us abounding life—life which is characterised by trust, and peace, and rest, and joy, and love, and power, and victory. We are as unable to live this life in our own strength as we were unable, in the first instance, to save ourselves by our own efforts; but He who began a good work in us can and will perfect it in all who yield to Him. A mechanistic psychology denies what it cannot explain, but the joyful experience and witness of a host of Christians, from the apostolic age to the present time, has been that "the law of the Spirit of life in Christ Jesus hath made us free from the law of sin and death."

If one is living before Easter, the Christ of the New Testament is not in his experience at all: he is spiritually dead. If one is living between Easter and Pentecost, Christ is in his experience as Redeemer and Saviour: he has spiritual life. But not unless one is living from and in Pentecost is the Lordship of Christ a reality to him, or can he enjoy spiritual health, which is holiness.

No one can but be impressed by observing the change which Pentecost wrought in the experience of the apostles. In the betweentime from Easter to Pentecost two things characterised them: fear, and a lost sense of vocation. We see them first behind closed doors for fear of the Jews, and then later, Peter, who had been called to high apostleship, said, "I go a fishing!" and the others said, "We also go with thee." No one can live the abounding life who is in the grip of fear, or who has failed or ceased to believe that God has for him a programme of life.

This between experience has been the trouble from the beginning. It is illustrated by Israel in the wilderness between Egypt and Canaan, and by Paul's subjection to self, between his deliverance from the guilt of sin and his freedom from its power, as set forth in the Roman letter. It is this that is taught by the apostle's threefold analysis of men as "natural," and "carnal," and "spiritual." The "natural man" has not reached Calvary at all; the "carnal man" is on the right side of the cross, but has not reached Pentecost; and the "spiritual man" has entered by Pentecost into the Kingdom which is "righteousness, and peace, and joy in the Holy Spirit." The carnal Christian has spiritual life, for he is spoken of as a "babe in Christ," but there is little

or no spiritual growth. He is like Lazarus, who, though raised
from the dead, was yet "bound hand and foot with grave-
clothes" until deliverance came. Is not this sadly illustrative
of the experience of many Christians, people who are in bondage
to fear, or doubt, or self, or sin? Yet freedom is our inheritance;
we are called to the liberty of the sons of God. It will be a great
day for each of us when we penitently acknowledge that we have
not been what it has been God's purpose to make us; and it will
be a greater day when we dare to believe that we may become all
that it is in His power to make us.

It is this aspect of truth which Keswick exists to emphasise.
The movement is not ignorant of, nor indifferent to, the social
implications and obligations of the Gospel; but it is held and
taught that the value of our outward activities is determined by
the reality and depth of our inward experience; that it is the man
who is entirely right with God who is best qualified and equipped
to help his fellow men. It was not until after Pentecost that the
disciples socially applied the Gospel; and it was not until after
Pentecost that they were fired with enthusiasm and determination
to carry the Good News to all mankind, whatever the cost might
be: and ever since then, the Church's greatest days have been
when she has lived and wrought in the power of Pentecost,
which is normal Christianity. The Christian Church has plant,
and organisation, and money, and learning, and much besides;
but all this can be of no avail if she lacks Pentecostal power. We
have banked more on prestige than on prayer; we have organised
more than we have agonised; we have allowed ritual to obscure
reality; we have thought more of conferences than of consecration:
in short, we have displaced the Holy Spirit, and it is high time
that we recognised the cause of our spiritual stringency.

The way out, and only way out, is by a return to Pentecost,
which is the source and secret of abounding life.

But nothing effective will be done so long as we think in terms
of the Church as a whole. We must be personal if we would be
practical, for the Christian Church is only the aggregate of all
Christians, and it cannot be better than the spiritual experience
of those who compose it. The experience of Christians is not
necessarily Christian experience. Christian experience is what the
New Testament reveals, what Christ by His holy Passion has made
possible, and what the Holy Spirit yielded to makes actual: but
the experience of Christians is, too often, one of dispeace, of joy-
lessness, of prayerlessness, of worldliness, and of defeat: and can
anyone imagine that such an experience as that is Christianity!
If Christ has called us to holiness of life, it is because He has made
it possible; and if we will dare to believe that, and to draw upon

our resources in Him, we shall experience in our hearts and demonstrate to others the reality of abounding life.

The sum, then, of what we have endeavoured to say is just this, that it is the intention of God that Christ shall be not only Saviour, but also our Lord; that we shall be not only justified, but also sanctified; that we shall be delivered not only from sin's guilt, but also from its power; that we shall not only live, but live triumphantly.

By Christ's death and resurrection, apprehended and trusted, we enter into eternal life; and by whole-hearted yieldedness to Christ as Lord and Master, we enter into the experience of abounding life. The yieldedness becomes a reality when, renouncing all known sin, and looking to Christ to accomplish in and through us by His Spirit, what by His death He has made possible, we follow on in love and obedience.

The evidence and expression of such an attitude will be in Christlikeness of character, and in sacrificial service for men. For the exhibition of such a life as that, the world is waiting; and surely the experience of such a life must be the devout desire of each of us. Then let us believe Christ when He says He came that we might live like that; and let us believe that He has given to us His Holy Spirit for its realisation. Here and now in this evening hour, let us claim our inheritance.

We need not wait for Him. He is waiting for us. In this place and moment He is offering Himself to us as the source of strength and satisfaction, as well as the place of safety; and if we will but receive Him, fear will be exchanged for trust, doubt for certainty, ineffectiveness for success, defeat for victory, and sadness for joy. We have tried trying and have failed; why not now try trusting? We have wrought in our own strength and have found it to be weakness; why not now take hold of His strength? The faith we once exercised for the possession of divine life, let us now exercise for the experience of abounding life; and as Christ met us then, so He will meet us now. May our attitude in the quiet of this tent, in this evening hour, be one not of yearning, but of yielding; not of struggling, but of resting; not of asking, but of taking. Let us go out to live the abounding life. May it be so, for His Name's sake.

THE CARNAL CHRISTIAN

ANDREW MURRAY was a Dutch Reformed pastor in South Africa who wrote many inspirational books, including *Abide in Christ* and *With Christ in the School of Prayer.*

THE CARNAL CHRISTIAN

REV. DR. ANDREW MURRAY

And I, brethren, could not speak unto you as unto spiritual, but as unto carnal, even as unto babes in Christ—I CORINTHIANS 3: 1–4.

THE apostle commences the chapter by telling these Corinthians that there are two stages of Christian experience. Some Christians are *carnal*, some are *spiritual*. By the discernment which God's Spirit gave the apostle, he saw that the Corinthians were carnal, and he wanted to tell them so. You will find the word "carnal" four times in these four verses.

The apostle felt that all his preaching would do no good if he talked about spiritual things to men who were unspiritual. They were Christians, real Christians, babes in Christ; but there was one deadly fault—they were carnal. So the apostle seems to say, "I cannot teach you spiritual truth about the spiritual life; you cannot take it in." But that was not because they were stupid. They were very clever, full of knowledge, but unable to understand spiritual teaching. That teaches us this simple lesson: that all the trouble in the Church of Christ among Christians who sometimes get a blessing and lose it again is just because they are carnal; and all that we need if we want to keep the blessing is that we become spiritual. We must choose what style of Christian life we should like to live—the carnal life, or the spiritual. Choose the spiritual, and God will be delighted to give it you. O God, help us all to say tonight, "Lord, make me a spiritual man. Fill me with Thy Spirit."

Now if we are to understand this teaching we must begin by trying thoroughly to know what this carnal state is, and I think I shall be able to point you to four very marked characteristics of the carnal state. The first thing I have to say about it is that *the carnal state is a state of protracted infancy*. It is a time ago since you were converted, and you ought to have been a young man by this time, but you are still a babe in Christ. "I have fed you with milk and not with meat; for hitherto you were not able to bear it." You know what a babe is, and what a beautiful thing babyhood is. You cannot have a more beautiful little thing than

21

a child six months old, with its ruddy cheeks, its laughing and smiling face, the kicking of its little feet, and the movement of its little fingers. What a beautiful object! But suppose I saw such a child, and came back after six months and the child was not a bit bigger, the parents would begin to say, "We are afraid there is something the matter; the child won't grow." And if after three years I came back and saw there the baby no bigger yet, I should find the parents sad. They would tell me, "The doctor says there is some terrible disease about the child; it cannot grow. He says it is a wonder it is alive, and yet it does live." I come back after ten years, and there is that helpless infant, and still there is no growth.

You see, babyhood at the proper time is the most beautiful thing in the world, but babyhood continued too long is a burden and a sorrow, a sign of disease. Corinthian Christians. They continued babes. Now, what are the marks of a babe? There are specially two marks: a babe cannot help itself, and a babe cannot help others. First, *a babe cannot help itself*; and that is the life of many Christians. They make their ministers spiritual nurses of babes. It is a solemn thing that these spiritual babes keep their ministers occupied all the time in nursing them and feeding them, and they never want to grow to be men, and they never help themselves. They do not know themselves how to feed on Christ's Word, and the minister must feed them. They do not know what contact with God is; the minister must pray for them. They do not know what it is to live as those who have God to help them; they always want to be nursed.

Do take care that that does not become the reason why *you* come to the Convention—to get your nurses to give you spiritual meat. God be praised for the preaching of the Gospel, and for the fellowship of the Convention. But, oh, you know what baby does: baby always keeps the house going, and very often mother cannot go out because there is baby, or the servant must be there to keep baby, or the nurse must be there; but baby always occupies somebody. You cannot leave him alone. So there are many spiritual infants to whom ministers are always going, and who are always wanting some help. Instead of allowing themselves to be trained up to know their God and be strong, alas, it is a protracted infancy. They cannot help themselves, but occupy others. Is not that just what we read in the epistle to the Hebrews? There was the very same condition; we read that those who had been so long converted, and who ought to have been teachers, needed themselves to be taught the very rudiments of Christianity. And there are, as I have said, people who are always wanting to be helped, instead of being a help to others.

For a little child, a spiritual babe of three months old, to be carnal, and not to know altogether what sin is, and not yet to have got victory, is, as Paul says, a thing not to be wondered at. But when a man continues year after year in the same state of always being conquered by sin, there is something radically wrong. Nothing can keep a child in protracted infancy but disease of some sort. And if we have to say continually, "I am not spiritual," then do let us say, "O God, I am carnal; I am in a diseased state, and want to be helped out of it."

The second mark of a carnal state is that *sin and failure prove master.* Sin has the upper hand. What proof does Paul give that those people were carnal? He first charges them, and then he asks them a question. "Among you there are envyings and strifes and divisions; are ye not carnal?" And then again, "One says, I am of Paul, and another, I am of Apollos, and another, I am of Cephas." Are ye not carnal? asks Paul in effect; is not that evident? You act just like other men; you are not acting like heavenly, renewed men, who live in the power and love of the Holy Ghost. Oh, friends, you know that God who loveth us dwelleth in light, and that love is the great commandment, and that the Cross of Christ is the evidence of God's love, and that the first-fruit of the Holy Spirit is love. The whole of John's Gospel means love: and when men give way to their tempers and pride and envying and divisions; when you hear people saying sharp things about others; when a man cannot open out his whole heart and face to a brother who has done him wrong, and forgive him; when a woman can speak about her neighbour with contempt as "That wretched thing," or say to another, "Oh, how I dislike that woman"—all these are fruits of the carnal spirit. Every touch of unlovingness is nothing but the flesh. Most of you know that the word *carnal* is a form of the Latin word for *flesh*, and all unlovingness is nothing but the fruit or work of the flesh. The flesh is selfish and proud and unloving; therefore every sin against love is nothing but a proof that the man is carnal.

You say, "I have tried to conquer it, but I cannot." That is what I want to impress upon you. Do not try, while you are in the carnal state, to bear spiritual fruit. You must have the Holy Spirit in order to love God, and then the carnal will be conquered. He will give you the spirit to do the right.

And it is not only true of the sins against love; there are so many other sins. Take worldliness, which somebody says has "honeycombed the Church." Take the love of money; take the pursuit of business, making people sacrifice everything to the increase of riches. Take so much of our life, the seeking after luxury and pleasure and position. What is all that but the flesh?

It gratifies the flesh; it is exactly what the world thinks desirable and delights in. And if you live like the world it is a proof that the spirit of the world, which is in the flesh, is in you. The carnal state is proved by the power of sin.

Someone asked me yesterday, "How about the want of love of prayer?" He wanted to know how the art of loving fellowship with God could be attained. I said, "My brother, that cannot be attained in any way until you discover that it must come outside of the carnal state. The flesh cannot delight in God; that is your difficulty. You must not say or write down a resolution in your journal that 'I will pray more.' You cannot force it; but let the axe come to the root of the tree. Cut down the carnal mind. How can you cut it down? *You* cannot. But let the Holy Spirit of God come with the condemnation of sin and the Cross of Christ. Give over the flesh to death, and the Spirit of God will come in. Then you will learn to love prayer and love God, and love your neighbour, and you will be possessed of humility and spiritual-mindedness and heavenly-mindedness. The carnal state is the root of every sin."

I come to the next point. If we want to know this carnal state thoroughly, we must take special notice that *the carnal state can co-exist with great spiritual gifts*. Remember, there is a great difference between spiritual gifts and spiritual graces, and that is what many people do not understand. Among the Corinthians, for instance, there were very wonderful spiritual gifts. In the first chapter Paul says, "I thank my God . . . that ye are enriched in all utterance and knowledge." That was something wonderful to praise God for. And in the second epistle he says, in effect, "You do not come behind in any gift; see that you have the gift of liberality also." And in the twelfth chapter, he speaks about the gifts of prophecy, and of faith that could remove mountains, and of knowledge, and of all mysteries, as things that they were ardently seeking for; but he tells them that these will not profit them unless they have love. They delighted in the gifts, and did not care for the graces. But Paul shows them a more excellent way—to learn to love and to be humble; that love is the greatest thing of all, for love is God-like above everything.

It is a very solemn thing for us to remember that a man may be gifted with prophecy, that a man may be a faithful and successful worker in some particular sphere among the poor and needy, and yet by the sharpness of his judgment and the pride that comes into him, and by other things, he may give proof that while his spiritual gifts are wonderful, spiritual graces are too often absent. Oh, take care that Satan does not deceive us with the thought, "I work for God, and God blesses me, and others look up to me, and I am the means of helping others." Beloved fellow Christians, that a carnal man may have spiritual gifts is unspeakably solemn, because it must bring the most earnest and successful man to his knees before God with the thought, "Am I not, after all that God's Spirit works in me as a matter of gift, possibly giving way to the flesh, in lack of humility or love or purity or holiness?" God search us and try us, for His Name's sake!

A further point is this, that *the carnal state renders it impossible for a man to receive spiritual truth.* That is of the utmost importance here at Keswick. You see, perhaps, hundreds of Christians hungering for the Word, and they listen, and they say, "What beautiful truths, what clear doctrines, what helpful expositions of God's Word!" And yet they do not get helped one step; or they get helped for two or three weeks, and the blessing passes away. What is the reason? There is an evil at the bottom; the carnal state is hindering the reception of spiritual truth.

I am afraid that in our churches we often make a terrible mistake. We preach to carnal Christians what is only fit for spiritual men, and they think it so beautiful, and they take it into their heads and delight in it and say, "That is grand. What a view of the truth that man can give!" Yet their lives remain unchanged; they are carnal, with all the spiritual teaching they get. If there is one thing that we ought each to ask God, it is this, "Lord, deliver me from taking up spiritual teaching into a carnal mind." The only evidence that you get a blessing at Keswick is that you are lifted out of the carnal into the spiritual state. God is willing to do it, and let us plead for it, and accept it.

Now comes the very important and solemn question: *Is it possible for a man to get out of the carnal into the spiritual state? And how is it possible?* I want to answer that, and to point out the steps which must be taken to that end. I want to say to every honest, earnest heart that is longing to be spiritual, You can get out of the carnal state tonight, into the spiritual state. And what is needed for that?

I think the first thing is that a man must have *some sight of the spiritual life, and some faith in it.* At bottom our hearts are so full of unbelief, without our knowing it, that we do not accept, as a settled matter, that we can become spiritual men. We do not believe it.

I heard a most interesting story just before I left the Cape. I was talking to a man of much Christian experience about my coming over to England, and I said to him, "Tell me, what is the state of the Christians in England? You have worked among them, and know them well." He replied, "I believe there is nothing so terrible among them as *unbelief*." Then he told me a story of a young man of high promise and great gifts, who was working in England for Christ. That young man had great gifts, but my friend could not understand why, with all those gifts, he did not get more blessing. Well, these two men spent a whole day in trying to find out what it was that was hindering the younger of them from being a greater blessing. The person to whom I spoke told me that his friend had to take a meeting that same night, but that he could not go to it as he felt so feeble, and the power of the world so strong. He was not assured that God was ready to give the blessing. So the other said, "I will take your meeting. Go home, and come back tomorrow morning at nine o'clock." He came back the next morning, and they began to speak and pray again, and in the course of the day the young man received a blessing from God; and since that time he has been ten times more blessed in his work than ever before. Oh, do believe that if you are ready and willing it is possible for God to make a spiritual man of you.

The Word speaks about two powers of life—the flesh, and the Spirit: the flesh, our life under the power of sin; the Spirit, God's life coming to take the place of our life. Some people have said to me, with respect to the death of self: "Oh, this is so hard to understand; do tell us what it is." I replied, "Do not try to understand it with your intellect. The death is in Him. He died for you, and He will give it to you if you yield yourselves utterly to Him." What we need, and what the Bible tells us, is to give our whole life, with every idea of strength or power, away unto death, to become nothing, and receive the life of Christ and of the Spirit to do all for us. Do believe that can be.

You say, "That is so high and holy and glorious, I do not think I can reach it." No, you cannot; but God will send it down to you. Your reaching up is the great danger; you cannot reach it. But if you believe that God wants, in a supernatural way, according to His everlasting love, to give you down from heaven the power of the Holy Spirit, then God will do for you more than you can ask or think.

I believe that it is possible for a man to live every day as led by the Holy Ghost. I have read in God's Word that God sheds abroad His love in the heart by the Holy Spirit. I have read in God's Word that as many as are led by the Spirit, they are the children of God. I have read in God's Word that if we are born again, we are to walk by the Spirit, or in the Spirit. Dear friends, it *is* possible; it is the life God calls you to and that Christ redeemed you for. As soon as He shed His blood, He went away to heaven to send the Spirit to His people. As soon as He was glorified, His first work was to give the Holy Spirit. If you will begin to believe in the power of Christ's blood to cleanse you, and in the power of the glorified Christ to give His Spirit in your heart, you have taken the first step in the right direction. Though you should feel ever so wretched, do hold fast to Jesus. He can fill you with the Spirit, for He has commanded you to "be filled with the Spirit." Will you not come tonight and say, "God helping me, I want to be a spiritual man"?

But secondly, it is not enough that a man should have a vision of that spiritual life which is to be lived; it is also very needful that a man should be *really convicted of his carnality*. This is a difficult, and solemn, but, as I say, needful lesson. There is a great difference between the sins of the unconverted man and the sins of the believer. As an unconverted man you had to be convicted of sin, and make confession of it; you all admit that. But what were you convicted of, chiefly? Of the grossness of sin; and very much of the guilt and punishment of sin. But there was very little conviction of inward, spiritual sins. You had no knowledge of them. There was very little conviction of inward sinfulness. God does not always give that, or ordinarily, in conversion. And so, how is a man to get rid of these two things—the vile sin, and the deep inner sinfulness? In this way: after he has become a Christian, God gives the Holy Spirit to convict him of the carnal, fleshly life; and then the man begins to mourn over it, and be ashamed of it, and cry out like Paul, "O wretched man that I am! I am a believer, but who shall deliver me from the body of this death?" He begins to turn round for help, and to ask, Where am I to get deliverance? He seeks it in many ways, by struggling and resolve; but he does not get it until he is brought to cast himself absolutely at the feet of Jesus. Do not forget that if you are to become a spiritual man, if you are to be filled with the Holy Ghost, it must come from God in heaven, who alone can do it.

How different our living and praying and preaching would be if the presence of the Holy One, who fills eternity, who fills the universe, were revealed to us! To that end God wants to bring us to a condition of utter brokenness. Somebody said to me, "It is dreadful, that call to *die*!" Yes, it is dreadful, if you had to do it in your own strength. But, oh, if you would only understand that God gave Jesus to die, and Jesus did it all, and God wants to plant you into Jesus that you may be delivered from the accursed power of the flesh. Oh, do believe that it is a blessing to be utterly broken down and utterly in despair, that you may learn to trust in God alone. Paul says somewhere, in effect, "I had the sentence of death in myself, that I might learn not to trust in myself but in God who raiseth the dead." That is the place you must come to under conviction of your carnality: "The flesh prevails and triumphs in me, and I cannot conquer it. Have mercy, my God! God help me!" And God *will*. Oh, become willing to bow before God in conviction and confession.

Then comes the third thing: and that is, to believe that *we can pass from the carnal to the spiritual condition in a moment of time*. People want to *grow out of* the carnal into the spiritual, and they never can. They seek more preaching and teaching in order, as they think, to grow out of the carnal into the spiritual. That babe that I spoke of, though ten years old, remained as big as a child of six months; it had got disease, and it wanted healing. Then growth would come. Now, the carnal state is a state of terrible disease. The carnal Christian is a babe in Christ. He is a child of God, Paul says, but he has this terrible disease, and consequently he cannot grow. How is the healing to come? It must come through God; and God longs to give it you this very hour.

Let me say here that a man who becomes a spiritual man tonight is not yet a man of spiritual maturity. I cannot expect from a young Christian, who has got the Holy Spirit in His fullness, what I can expect from a mature Christian who has been filled with Him for twenty years. There is a great deal of growth and maturity in the spiritual life. But what I speak of, when I speak of *one step*, is this: you can change your place, and instead of standing in the carnal life, enter the spiritual life.

Note the reason why the two expressions are used. In the carnal man there is something of the spiritual nature; but you know that bodies get their names from that which is their most prominent element. A thing may be used for two or three objects, but it will likely get its name from that which is most prominent. A thing may have several characteristics, but the name will be given according to that which is most striking. So, Paul says, in other words, to those Corinthians, "You babes in Christ are carnal; you are under the power of the flesh, giving way to temper and unloveliness, and not growing, or capable of receiving spiritual truth, with all your gifts." And the spiritual man is a man who has not reached final perfection; there is abundant room for growth. But if you look at him, the chief mark of his nature and conduct is that he is a man given up to the Spirit of God. He is not perfect, but he is a man who has taken the right position, and said, "Lord God, I have given myself to be led by Thy Spirit. Thou hast accepted me and blessed me, and the Holy Spirit now leads me." Do let us get hold of the thought that, God helping us, we can tonight leave our place on the one side, and take it on the other.

You may have heard the story that is often used in evangelistic services, about the man who was converted by a minister drawing a line and talking to him about it. He was a sick man, seventy years of age, and a minister visited him faithfully, and talked to him about the blood of Christ. "Oh, yes," responded the man, "I know about the blood of Christ, that it can save us; and about pardon; and that if God does not pardon us we cannot enter heaven." Yet the minister saw that the man had not the slightest sense of sin. Whatever the minister said, he said "Yes" to, and there was no life in it, no conviction of sin. And the minister tells us that when he himself was beginning to get into despair he one day prayed: "O God, help me to show this man his state." All at once a thought came into his mind. The floor of the man's room was strewn with sand, and the minister drew a line with his stick in the sand, and on the one side he wrote the words, "sin, death, hell," and on the other side, "Christ, life, heaven." The old man asked, "What are you doing?" The minister answered, "Listen! Do you think one of these letters on the left side could get up and go over the line to the right side?" "Of course not," was the answer. Then the minister said solemnly, "Just as little can a sinner who is on the left side get over to the right side. That line divides all mankind, and those who are saved are on the right side, and the unsaved are on the left side. It is Christ who must take you up from the left side and bring you to the right side. On what side are you?" There was no answer. The minister prayed with him, and went home praying that God would bless him. He went back the next day, and the question was, "Well, my friend, on what side are you?" He at once answered with a sigh, "On the wrong side." But it was not long before that man welcomed the Gospel and accepted Christ.

I would like tonight to draw a line straight through the centre of this hall, and ask all of you who believe and confess that God has given you His Holy Spirit to lead you, and who know what the joy of the Holy Ghost is, to take your places at the right-hand side. Then I would ask all you who have felt tonight that you are still carnal to come to the left side, and say, "O God, I confess that my Christian life is for the most part carnal, under the power of the flesh." Then I would plead with you, and tell you that you cannot save yourselves from the flesh, or get rid of it, but that if you come and accept Christ afresh, Christ can lift you over into the new life. You belong to Christ, and He belongs to you; what you need is just to cast yourselves upon Him,

HOW TO RECEIVE
THE HOLY GHOST

R. A. TORREY was a Congregationalist pastor who became superintendent of Moody Bible Institute in Chicago (1889–1908), then pastor of Moody Memorial Church in Chicago and the Church of the Open Door in Los Angeles (1913–24).

HOW TO RECEIVE THE HOLY GHOST

Rev. Dr. R. A. Torrey

Toward the close of a Convention in America—it was a Convention of Christian workers, who were speaking of the different forms of Christian work into which God had led them—a lady came to me and said, "Almost every worker who has spoken from that platform has said that the whole secret of God's blessing upon the work has been the baptism of the Holy Ghost which he had received. But," she said, "none of you have told us how to obtain the Holy Spirit. We want someone to tell us that before the Convention closes." It was a wise request, and it was heeded. That is my subject tonight—How to receive the Holy Ghost. But, before entering upon it, let me say that, no matter how definitely any of us may have received the Holy Spirit in the past—and, thank God, many of us have very definitely received the Holy Spirit in the past—we need a new infilling tonight, just as much as anyone who came to this Convention having never heard that there was such a Person as the Holy Spirit; and what is said will apply to us, just as much as it applies to the one who, for the first time, definitely received the Holy Spirit.

In other words, there is a very plain path, marked out so definitely in the Word of God that no one who looks for it need go astray, consisting of a few simple steps that anyone in this tent can take; and it is absolutely certain that, if you take those steps, you will receive the Holy Spirit. Now, that is very positive, isn't it, very dogmatic; but I would not dare to be so, if the Bible were not equally dogmatic. When the Bible is positive, what right have you and I to be shaky? People sometimes say to me, "You are a very dogmatic teacher," to which I reply, "I try to be so." I want to be just as positive as the Word of God. I do not think I am so, but that is my ambition—to be just as positive as the Bible. What right has a minister of the Gospel to be any less positive than the message that God has given to him? We are men with a message; that message is in this Book, and when the Book asserts something positively, you and I have no right to put in "ifs" and "buts" and "perhaps" and "maybes" before it.

33

If anyone should come to me and say, "Can you tell me just what to do, and guarantee that, if I do it, I should be saved?" I should most certainly say, "Yes." If I could not tell anybody what to do, and guarantee them that, if they do it, they would be saved instantly, I should have no right to preach the Gospel. But if they come to me and say, "Can you tell me just what to do, and guarantee that, if I do it, I should receive the Holy Spirit?" equally positively I should say, "Yes." In Acts 2:38 you will find the path laid down. All the simple steps are in this verse. I shall refer to other verses later, just simply as throwing light upon this; but all the steps are here. "Then Peter said unto them, repent, and be baptised every one of you in the name of Jesus Christ for the remission of sins, and ye shall receive the gift of the Holy Ghost." That is just as positive as I was. Peter says, "You do these things, and the result will be that ye shall receive the Holy Ghost"; and so I say, if you do these things you shall receive the gift of the Holy Ghost.

Now, what are the things to be done? The *first two steps* are in the word "Repent." Repent, what does it mean? You have been told, over and over again, that repentance is a change of mind; and when you are told that, you are told the truth. Repentance is a change of mind; but a change of mind about what? About God, about sin, about Jesus Christ. What a change of mind is about, in any given instance, has to be determined by the context. In this case, the context clearly shows that the change of mind is, primarily, about Jesus Christ. We are told, in Acts 2: 36, that Peter said to those who were around him, "That same Jesus, whom ye have crucified, God hath made both Lord and Christ.' And the next verse says, "When they heard this, they were pricked in their heart," as well they might be, "and said, men and brethren, what shall we do?" And Peter replied, "You have crucified your Lord and Christ. Change your mind about Him; change from the mind that crucifies Him, to the mind that accepts Him." That is the first step—to accept Jesus as your Saviour and your Lord.

"Well," some will say, "all of us in this tent have done that already." Have you? I wish I knew that you have. Have you accepted Christ as your Saviour? "Why," you say, "most assuredly. We are all church members, or members of chapels." That doesn't prove it. What is it to accept Christ as a Saviour? To accept Christ as a Saviour is to rest all your hope of acceptance before God, upon the finished work of Christ on the cross of Calvary. Have you done it? If I should go down the aisles of this tent, and stop at the end of each row, and put to you the question, "Are you saved?" I presume most of you would reply,

"Yes, I am saved." But then, if I should put to you a second question: "On what are you depending for salvation?" I should get a variety of answers. Some of you would reply something like this: "I have united with the Church; I have been baptised; I have been confirmed; I say my prayers regularly; I read my Bible every day; I try to work and do something for Christ; I give a tithe of my income to the Lord's work; I go to church regularly, and I try to live just as near right as I know how. That is what I am depending upon for salvation." If it is, you are not saved. All of those things are your works—good and proper in their place, but your works; and the Word of God distinctly asserts that "by the works of the law shall no flesh living be justified in His sight." But if I should go to others, they would reply like this: "I am not depending upon anything that I ever did, nor upon anything that I am ever going to do. I am depending upon what Jesus Christ did, when He bore my sin in His own body on the cross." Well, you are on the right line. If that is true, you have received, you have taken Christ as your Saviour, and you have taken the first step to receiving the Holy Spirit.

The apostle Paul says, in Galatians 3: 2, writing to the believers in Galatia, "Received ye the Spirit by the works of the law, or by the hearing of faith?" You remember the circumstances. Paul was passing through Galatia, and was overtaken by some physical extremity. We are not told what it was, but the indication is that it was some trouble with his eyes. Whatever it may be, he was stopped by physical infirmity. But he went on preaching, as he did every time he had opportunity, unless the Holy Spirit stopped him. He preached to the people of Galatia the finished work of Christ—that Christ had redeemed them from the curse of the law, being made a curse in their place. They believed him, and were saved, and God set His seal to their conversion by giving them the Holy Spirit. But Paul moved on, and certain men came down from Jerusalem, saying, "This is not enough, to believe on Christ. You must keep the Mosaic law, you must be circumcised according to the law of Moses"; just as certain men come around in our day and say, "You must keep the Mosaic seventh-day Sabbath." It is the old controversy breaking out afresh. Paul heard of it. The young converts were turned upside down, as some are nowadays, by legalisers. Paul heard of it, and his righteous soul was stirred within him. He wrote this wonderful epistle to the Galatians, and he said, first, "Why, Abraham himself, in whom you make your boast, was justified by simply believing God, before he was ever circumcised. He was circumcised after he was justified, simply as a seal of the faith that he had while still being in uncircumcision." Then he appealed to their own experience. "Now," said he, "look here: you men received the Holy Spirit. How did you receive Him? By keeping the Mosaic law? or by the simple hearing of faith of the testimony of God regarding Jesus, believing in Him and in His finished work?" "Oh, Paul, we see it. How ever could we be so deceived? Why, we received the Holy Spirit by the simple hearing of faith, by believing God's testimony about Christ, and by trusting in Him." It is so today. The gift of the Holy Ghost is God's seal upon those who look up from themselves and their own works utterly, and look to the one work of Christ when He died upon the cross of Calvary, for you and for me.

I had a deacon in my church, a Scotsman, well versed in the Scriptures. One day he was crossing the railway track to the south of Chicago. On the engine was a young convert, and just as he was going over the crossing he saw John Morrison standing on the side, and said, "John, don't you want a lift?" "Yes," says John. "Then get up into the cab." Morrison got up into the cab, and at once began to draw the young convert out. After they had talked a little while, Morrison said to him, "You have a different religion from mine." "John, what do you mean? I thought we both had the same religion." "No," John says, "you have a different religion from mine. Yours is a religion of two letters; mine is a religion of four letters." "John, what do you mean?" "Well, your religion is D-O, do; you are all the time talking about what you do. My religion is D-O-N-E, done. I am resting in what Jesus Christ has done when He bore my sin in His own body on the cross." Friends, what are you looking at? At your doing, or at what He has done? The *first step* is to believe the testimony of God about Jesus Christ, that every one of your sins was laid upon Christ; and to trust God to pardon you, not because of anything you ever did or are ever going to do, but because of what Jesus did when He died in your place on the cross of Calvary. Then, you must receive Him, not only as your Saviour, but as your Lord. I shall come to that again, under another passage.

The *second step* is in the word "repent"—a change of mind about sin; a change of mind from the attitude of mind that loves and indulges in sin, to that attitude of mind that hates sin. Or, to put it into the language of action, the second step is to renounce sin. The Holy Spirit is the *Holy* Spirit; and you cannot have Him, and sin. It is either the Holy Spirit or sin; and, as long as you hold on to one little fragment of sin, you cannot have Him. Friends, we touch here upon the root of the difficulty in thousands of lives. People come to conventions like this, to get blessing, and they think they will get blessing from listening to the speakers; but they want to get the blessing without judging their sin. You cannot do it. People pray, and pray, and pray for the Holy Spirit, but they do not give up sin. You can pray, if you will, until the Lord comes; and you will get no blessing, if you hold on to your sin. But you can get the blessing in two seconds, if you give up your sin. Why, people write to me and say, "I have been praying for the baptism of the Holy Spirit." They use different forms of language, but it means the same thing. I am not concerned about phrases. "I have been praying for the baptism of the Holy Spirit"—one man said five, another ten, another man twenty years—"but I don't get on. What is the trouble?" When people say that to me, I am generally led to look square into their eyes, and to say, "My brother, my sister, it is *sin*." And, if I could look into your heart as God does at this moment, I could put my finger upon the specific sin. Sometimes it is what you call "a very small one." There are no small sins. Every sin is an act of rebellion against God. Mr. Charles G. Finney tells about a woman who was greatly concerned upon this subject. She would stay up all night after the meetings were over, praying for the baptism of the Spirit. Her friends feared that she would become insane from the intensity of her anxiety. One night she went home from the meeting, knelt down, and began to pray for the baptism of the Spirit. As she prayed, some little matter of head adornment—something that I do not suppose would trouble anyone in this tent—the matter of controversy between that woman and God, came up. As it did so, she took the pins out of her hair, threw the thing across the room, and said, "There, go!" Instantly the power of God fell upon her.

Brothers and sisters, if you are praying, and are getting nothing for it, I tell you what to do: honestly ask God to show you if there is anything in your life, anywhere, that is displeasing in His sight; and then wait, listen, and give God time. If He doesn't show you anything after a time, then conclude that there is nothing; but don't be in too much of a hurry. If He does show you something, have done with it then and there. If there is anything that comes up every time when you get nearest to God, that is the difficulty. I said this down in Georgia, awhile ago. The Chairman of the Convention said, "Look over yonder." He didn't point, but he called attention to one at the side of the Tabernacle, and said, "That man is a minister of a denomination in North Georgia, which is not in sympathy with us along these lines. I am glad he is here." The man came day after day. At the last meeting—that at which I said what I am saying tonight—I found the man waiting in the vestibule. He said to me, "I didn't get up this afternoon, when you gave the invitation to do so." "I noticed that you didn't," said I. He replied, "I thought you said you didn't want anyone to stand up, unless it were one wholly surrendered to God, and holding nothing back." "That was just what I said." "Well, I could not say it." "Then you did perfectly right; I didn't want you to lie." "You hit me pretty hard this afternoon." "That is what I am here for." "You said that if anything always comes up every time we get nearest to God, that is the thing to deal with. Well, there *is* something that always comes up every time *I* get nearest to God. I'm not going to tell you what it is, but I think you know." "I think I do; I can smell it." "Well, that's all right; I thought I would tell you." That was on the Friday. I went down to Augusta, Georgia, the same day, and came through Atlanta on the following Tuesday. There I saw the Chairman of conference at the station as I passed through. He had been at the preachers' meeting, and now said, "Yesterday, the man I pointed out to you, stood up, having dealt with his sin, and surrendered himself to God, and he said, 'Brethren, I have been all wrong on this subject.' Then he told them what he had done, and continued, 'I have received a more definite blessing than I received when I was converted.'" It will be so with some of you, if you will judge your sin, if you will deal with your sin, if you will put away your sin. But if you try to excuse your sin, you will go away empty. If you try to make out that your sin is not so bad as someone else would make out, you will go away empty. But if you deal mercilessly with your own sin, you will get the blessing.

The *third step* is in this same verse, "Repent, and be baptised every one of you in the name of Jesus Christ." There must be an open confession of Christ before the world. If one has never been baptised in the past, either as an adult or in infancy, one should be baptised. I never felt the importance of baptism as I did in India. In other words, baptism is the crucial question in India. People there will go a great way—they will come to your meetings, they will tell you that they believe in your Christ, they will read your Bible, they will sympathise with you, and will give you money for your work; but they will not come right out, and be baptised as Christians. Why? Because the moment they do so it severs them from Hinduism, and makes them outcasts. I never felt the force of it as I did in India. But suppose that a person has been baptised already, as an adult or in infancy; even then, there should be an open confession of your own acceptance of what baptism signifies —the renunciation of sin, and identification with Jesus Christ. The baptism of the Holy Ghost is not for the secret disciple; it is for the openly-confessed follower of Jesus Christ. Everywhere that

we have gone in our missions over England, we have insisted upon
a public confession of acceptance of Christ, on the part of everyone who professes to be converted. People have come, and have
said to me, "You make it too hard."

Dr. George Wilson, of Edinburgh—he is here now—said to me
last night, "There is one thing I thank God for, about your
mission in Edinburgh—that you made it hard; that you insisted
upon open confession. Some brethren said that you made it too
hard; but I said, 'No, we want thoroughness.'" But, friends, we
not only insist upon open confession of Christ, on the part of the
young convert; we insist upon, and give opportunity for, confession of Christ upon the part of people who, in their hearts,
have been believers for years, but have never told anybody about
it. England is full of them—church members, and members of
chapels, who have never publicly stood up, faced the world, and
said, "I have taken Jesus as my Saviour, as my Lord, as my King."
All over England today there are people rejoicing in having
received the Holy Spirit, who didn't know Him twelve months
ago; because, although in their hearts they had accepted Christ,
perhaps years ago, they had never publicly confessed Him before
the world. If you have never openly confessed Christ, take the
first opportunity of doing it.

The *fourth step* is in Acts 5: 32, "We are His witnesses of these
things," says Peter; "and so is also the Holy Ghost whom God hath
given to them"—what?—"that obey Him." That is the fourth
step—*obedience*. It is in the first step. Obedience—I believe we
touch the very heart of the matter here. What is obedience?
"Why," you say, "obedience is doing what God tells you." Very
well, that is true; but that means doing *all* that God tells you.
Ah, here's the rub—doing all that God tells you! The heart of
obedience is in the will. Obedience, in its essence, is absolute
surrender to God. It is coming to God, and saying, "Heavenly
Father, here I am. I am Thy property; Thou hast bought me
with a price, and I acknowledge Thy ownership. Now, send me
where Thou wilt, do with me what Thou wilt, use me as Thou
wilt." Don't you remember that, in the Old Testament types
and symbols, it was when the whole burnt-offering was brought
to God and laid upon the altar—absolutely nothing withheld,
within or without—that then the fire of God came forth from the
Holy Place where God dwelt, and He accepted the gift? It is
when we come, as whole burnt-offerings, holding absolutely
nothing back, laying everything we have and are upon the altar,
that the fire of God falls. And it is going to fall in every heart
in this tent, which does that. Ah, but that is just what a great
many of you are afraid to do! I know of nothing at which men

tremble as they do at the thought of absolute surrender. People can go a great way, and yet stop short of absolute surrender. They may even turn to the foreign mission field, and confront all its hardships. I have had large experience of foreign missionaries, and can say that the talk about the foreign missionary living in luxury, is all nonsense. I wish those who talk like that would go and try it for a while. It is a hard life; it is a life of denial, in any place where I have ever been. But a great many men and women will go so far as to leave home, friends, and associations dear, and to go and confront all the hardships of the foreign missionary's life, and yet will stop short of absolute surrender. Foreign missionary after foreign missionary in Japan, China and India has told me frankly, "We have not yet come to the place of absolute surrender." A great many of you have an idea that, if you should say to God, "I surrender all," God would ask some hard thing of you, some ridiculous thing of you; and you hold back. When I was at Northfield one time, a gentleman came and said to me, "You must not talk upon absolute surrender. The men and women in this hall will have a fright, thinking that God may take away husbands from wives and parents from children, may require all sorts of hard things from them." I did speak upon it, and I said, "Who is your God? He certainly is not the God of the Bible." The name of the God of the Bible is what? Love; and absolute surrender to God, is simply absolute surrender to infinite Love. God is a Father.

Suppose that, for some time, I should be away, and should come back home suddenly. My boy hears me at the door, comes running down the stairs, and throws himself into my arms, as he surely would. Supposing he should say, "Father, I am so glad you are back; we didn't expect you so soon. Sit down and write me out a programme for the day. I'm going to do what you tell me, at every turn." It would be a red-letter day, and I'd sit down and make that programme right off. Should I sit down, call my wife, say, "Clara, what are the things that Reuben doesn't like to do?" and then write them down? Don't you know that I wouldn't? No; I would make that day the gladdest that Reuben Torrey, junr., ever saw in all his life! When you and I surrender to our Father, He brings into play all the resources of infinite love, and wisdom, and power, to fill your life and mine with sunshine. He may ask us to do things which we should not otherwise have chosen to do; but they will be the sweetest things we have to do. I refused to be a Christian for about six years, because I felt bound not to preach. I said, "I shall be a lawyer," and I deliberately refused Christ, because I was bound not to preach. When conversion did come, I *had* to preach; that is just what

Christ asked me to do; my whole conversion turned upon that. I didn't say, "I accept Christ," but I said, "I'll preach the Gospel." Today, friends, I'd rather preach the glorious Gospel than do anything else on earth! People come and say, "Aren't you tired, preaching five or six times a day?" No, I don't know anything so restful, so gloriously joyful, as preaching. I'd rather preach than eat! So it will be with you. God may ask you to do things you would not have chosen to do; but they will be the sweetest, gladdest things you have to do. However that may be, you will never receive the Holy Spirit until you do surrender all.

At a conference in America, a Presbyterian minister, prominent in his part of the country, and upwards of sixty years of age, came and wanted to see me alone, and we went to my room. He said, "Two university students from my church went to Northfield this midsummer, and heard you speak upon the baptism of the Holy Spirit. They came back home, called upon me and said, 'Pastor, we want to talk with you,' and they began to tell me what they had heard at Northfield. 'Pastor, we have heard something you do not know about'." I think that was rather impertinent on the part of the young men; but their man was real, and he said, "If you have, I want to hear about it now." The prominent minister sat there, while the two university students told him what they had heard. He said to me, "When they had gone, I took my hat and went off into the woods, where I found a great tree lying prostrate. I sat down upon the tree, took off my hat, and said, 'Heavenly Father, if those young men have something that I have not, I want it. Now, Father, the best I know, I surrender everything to Thee. Give me Thy Spirit'." He said to me, "Then I was quiet; and there came stealing into my heart the most wonderful peace I had ever known."

Oh, friends, *this tent is full of God!* This tent is full of the presence of the Holy Spirit, pressing upon every heart; and the moment you shoot back the bolts and open the door, He will fill in; and you will shoot back the bolts by absolute surrender. Some of you have been fighting for years. You have come to Keswick year after year; absolute surrender has been preached, and you have *almost* made it, but you have *not* made it. You have gone back home, and you have said, "I wonder why people have been so blessed at Keswick, while I have not." That is why you have not. Right now—do not wait until I have finished, do not wait until the after-meeting—right now, look up and say (and mean it), "I surrender all."

The *next step*, Luke 11: 13, "If ye then, being evil, know how to give good gifts unto your children, how much more shall your

heavenly Father give the Holy Spirit to them that *ask* Him?"
It is simply asking; definite prayer, for definite blessing. Many
people—good people—tell us that we ought not to pray for the
Holy Spirit. Well, Jesus Christ says that we should do so. They
reason it out very speciously. They say to you, "Christ gave the
Holy Spirit to the Church at Pentecost. Why pray for what the
Church already has?" To which Dr. Gordon, of Boston, replied,
"God gave Jesus Christ to the world, at Calvary. 'God so loved
the world that He gave His only begotten Son, that whosoever
believeth in Him should not perish, but have everlasting life.'
But what God gave to the world at Calvary, each individual in
the world has to appropriate to himself. And what God gave to the
Church at Pentecost, each individual in the Church has to appropriate to Himself; and God's way of appropriation, is prayer."
But they go further. "Every believer already has the Holy Spirit."
That is true, in a sense. "Then, why pray for what you already
have?" To which the simple answer is: it is one thing to have the
Holy Spirit dwelling, as every believer has, away back in some
hidden sanctuary, away back of consciousness, but nevertheless
there; and it is something gloriously more to have the Holy Spirit
taking complete possession of the temple. That comes in answer
to prayer. And, friends, even if we could not answer most of
their specious arguments, we take the simple words of Jesus Christ,
"How much more shall your heavenly Father give the Holy Spirit
to them that ask Him."

Once, at Boston Convention, a gentleman came to me, an
earnest Christian man apparently, saying, "According to the
programme this afternoon you speak on the baptism of the Holy
Spirit." "Yes, it is the most important subject on the programme." "I think it is important. Be sure and tell them not
to pray for the Holy Spirit." I said, "My brother, I shall be sure
and *not* tell them that; for Jesus says, 'How much more shall
your heavenly Father give the Holy Spirit to them that ask
Him'." "Oh, yes; but that was before Pentecost." "Certainly
after. Take it and read it." "'And when they had prayed,
the place was shaken where they were assembled together; and
they were all filled with the Holy Ghost, and they spake the
word of God with boldness.'" "How about Acts 8: 15, 16—
was it before or after Pentecost?" "Certainly after." "Take it
and read it." "Who (Peter and John), when they were come
down, prayed for them, that they might receive the Holy Ghost:
(for as yet He was fallen upon none of them)." Before Pentecost
and after, by specific statement and by illustrative example, the
Holy Spirit is given in answer to definite prayer.

But friends, with me it is not a question of experience. If it were, I would believe it. If I found anything taught in the Bible, with its interpretation in the context, I would believe it, whether I had experienced it or not. I do not believe in bringing the Bible down to the level of our experience, but I believe in bringing our experience up to the level of the Bible. So, if it were in the Bible, I would believe it, whether I had any experience of it or not. But, thank God I have experience of it; and I know that God gives the Holy Spirit in answer to prayer. I know it, just as well as I know that I stand here. How often, as I have prayed with an individual believer and brother, as we prayed, definitely and consciously, the Holy Spirit came upon us. How often, in our all-night prayer meetings in Chicago, as we have prayed, the Holy Spirit came upon us. I shall never forget one night in the vestry of our church. We had been having meetings of the ministers, at noon, preliminary to Mr. Moody coming to Chicago. I happened to be presiding at the meetings in the Y.M.C.A. Hall. One day a Baptist minister sprang to his feet, and said, "Brother Torrey, what we need in Chicago is an all-night prayer meeting of the ministers." "Very well, Mr. Emmett, we will have one on Friday night at 10 o'clock. If God keeps us all night, we will stay all night; and we will stay as long as God keeps us." On the Friday night there were four or five hundred people gathered in the vestry of the church—not all ministers; there were a great many ministers, some laymen, and some women. If ever I was in a meeting that the devil made a dead set to spoil, it was there: and that kind of meeting would have his first attention. There were three men by the door, whose whole idea of vital godliness was pounding on a chair, and howling until every head in the building was splitting. When a brother suggested that they should do things decently and in order, they swore at the man who said it. Then a man jumped up among the people in a corner, shouting "I'm Elijah"; but he was not to blame, for he was crazy. There are several Elijahs over in America, and we could afford to spare some of them! But it is a poor prayer-meeting that can be spoiled by such things. We were there for a blessing, and we were going to have it, if we sat there all night. About twelve o'clock God gave us complete victory, for the discordant elements were gone or completely subdued. From that time onward, what a night we had! About 215 were anointed. While we were all upon our knees, suddenly there fell upon us an awesome, glorious silence. Nobody could pray, nobody could sing, nobody could speak. All you could hear was a subdued sobbing of unutterable joy, all over the building. I do not think anyone looked up; but it seemed to me that, if one should look up, one could fairly see the atmosphere trembling with the power of the Holy Ghost. There we waited I know not how long. It was a time of wonderment, a time of joy, a time of unutterable awe. God was there.

The following Sunday morning, one of the deacons of my church came to me, more than thirty hours after that wonderful time; and he could hardly speak yet; he was all of a tremble. He took my hand, and softly whispered, "Brother Torrey, I shall never forget yesterday morning, till my dying day!" Men went out of that building, in various directions. One left about three o'clock, to take the early train. He went down to Missouri, upon business, being a manufacturer. When his business was done, he said to the hotel proprietor, "Is there any meeting in town?" "Yes, there is one at the Cumberland Presbyterian Church. He was a Cumberland Presbyterian himself, and he went up to the church. When he got there he asked, "May I say a word?" and the minister replied, "Certainly." With the power of God upon him, that manufacturer began to talk. In a few days I received, daily, people from that place. Altogether, fifty-eight persons were converted while that man was talking. Another young fellow went out early in the morning, and took train for ——, and in a few days thirty-eight men and boys professed conversion. That young man afterwards went to Africa, and Spencer Walton testified that he was baptised with the Holy Ghost and with fire. He was accidentally killed last year, after a wonderful display of God's power in his missionary work. Another young student went to a place near Milwaukee for a short time, and I had letters from ministers asking, "Have you in your Institute a man named Samuel Johnson? A stranger of that name has been going into the soldiers' home and into the school-houses, preaching, and everywhere he goes there are conversions. We do not know who he is, but he says he is from the Bible Institute. Is he one of your students?" These men were found all over the world. I do not think there was any mission field in my tour round the world—Japan, Australia, New Zealand, China—where I have not met someone who was in that meeting, and had gone out of it burning with the fire of God. It was no guess-work, that baptism of the Holy Ghost. And, friends, God is willing to do the same here tonight.

Once more—the *last step*; the simplest, and yet, to many, the hardest to take. What is it? Simple faith. Friends, no matter how positive a promise may be, in the Bible, you will never realise it in personal experience until you believe it. Now take, for example, James 1: 5. God says most positively, "If any of you lack wisdom, let him ask of God, who giveth to all men liberally, and unbraideth not; and it shall be given him." Can anything be more positive than that? But listen, it goes on to say, "Only let him ask in faith, nothing doubting (R.V.): for he that doubteth is like the surge of the sea, driven by the wind and tossed. For let not that man think that he shall receive anything of the Lord." People accept Christ, people put away sin, people confess Christ, people surrender all, and people ask; but there is just one step left, and they do not take it. What is it? Simple belief. Mark 11: 24, "What things soever ye desire, when ye pray, believe that ye receive them, and ye shall have them." Friends, there is a faith that goes beyond expectation; there is a faith that puts out its hand and takes what it asks. That comes out in the Revised Version of Mark 11: 24, "All things whatsoever ye pray and ask for, believe that ye have received them, and ye shall have them." Believe it on God's naked word; and, after you have believed it simply because God says so, you will have it in actual experimental knowledge. But you say, "How can I?" 1 John 5: 14, 15, answers the question. John says: "This is the confidence that we have in Him, that, if we ask anything according to His will, He heareth us: and, if we know that He hears us, whatsoever we ask, we know that we have the petitions that we have asked of Him."

Now, that is simple. When I go to God and offer a prayer, I then stop and say, "Was this prayer according to His will?" and if I find it promised in the Word, I know it is according to His will, for He said so. That is what the Bible is for—to tell of God's will. Therefore, I know that my prayer is heard. "And if we know that He hears us, whatsoever we ask," then I know that I have the thing that I have asked of Him. How? Because I feel it? No, because God says so. Having taken it on God's "say so," I afterwards get it in actual experience. Man's order is very different from God's order. Man's order is—the Word of God, then feeling, then faith. Never; it is according to man's belief in God's naked word. God's order is—His Word, believe because God says so; and, after that, feeling. Now apply this to the matter in hand. We kneel before God; we have taken the third step. We look up and say, "Heavenly Father, give me Thy Holy Spirit," or "baptise me with the Holy Spirit." Then stop. Is that according to His will? Luke 11: 13 says so. See also Acts 2: 39. Therefore, the thing we have asked is according to His will; and we read, "This is the confidence that we have in Him, that, if we ask anything according to His will, He heareth us." I read on, "And if we know that He hears us, whatsoever we ask, we know that we have the petitions that we have asked of Him." I know I have the petition I have asked of Him; He says so, here. What have I asked? The Holy Spirit. I know that I have the Holy

Spirit. Why? Because I feel it? Perhaps I shall, perhaps I shall not. I don't care whether I do or do not; but I know it, because 1 John 5: 15 says so. What I thus take in simple faith, I afterwards have in actual experimental knowledge.

Let me give you an illustration. Mr. Meyer (who is speaking over in the other tent tonight) and I were at a students' conference at Lake Geneva in America. Mr. Meyer spoke upon the subject with which I am dealing tonight, saying, "Young gentlemen, if any of you want to talk with us upon this matter, will you stay to the after meeting." Among them was a young man who had just graduated from one of our colleges. He said, "Mr. Torrey, I heard of this thirty days ago. I have been praying for the baptism of the Spirit ever since, but I do not get anything. What is the trouble?" I said, "Is your will laid down?" "I don't think it is." "Then," I said, "that is the trouble. Will you lay it down?" "I cannot." "Are you willing that God should lay it down for you?" "I am." "Let us kneel and ask Him to do it." I put two chairs together, and knelt down in the amphitheatre. He knelt down, and said, "Heavenly Father, empty me of my self-will, bring my will into conformity to Thine, lay my will down below it. I ask it in Jesus' name." "Is it done? It must be, because you have asked something according to His will"; and I opened the Bible at 1 John 5: 15. He repeated, "I have asked something according to His will; I know He has heard me, and therefore the thing is done." "Very well, now what is it you wish for?" "The baptism of the Holy Spirit." "Ask for it." He looked up and said, "Heavenly Father, baptise me with Thy Holy Spirit. I ask it in Jesus' name." I said, "Is it done?" He said, "I don't feel it." I said, "That is not what I asked you. Read the verses before you." He read, "This is the confidence that we have in Him, that, if we ask anything according to His will, He heareth us; and if we know that He heareth us, whatsoever we ask, we know that we have the petitions that we desired of Him." I said, "What is the confidence you have in Him?" "The confidence I have in Him is that, if I ask anything according to His will, He heareth me." "What did you ask?" "I asked the baptism of the Holy Spirit." I said, "Is that according to His will?" "Yes, Luke 11: 13, and Acts 2: 39 say so." "Very well," I said, "what do you know?" "I know that He heareth me." "Please read on." "And if we know that He hears us, whatsoever we ask, we know that we have the petitions that we have asked of Him." I said, "What do you know?" He said, "I know that I have the petition that I asked of Him." I said, "What did you ask?" He said, "I asked the baptism of the Holy Spirit." I said, "What do you know?" He said, "I know I have the baptism of the Holy Spirit. I don't feel it, but God says so." We arose, had a few words together, and next morning he took the early boat for the train to Chicago. He came back in a few days, and was sitting on my left in the amphitheatre. I turned and said, "Did you really receive the baptism of the Holy Spirit?" He scarcely needed to answer, for his face told the story; but he answered, "I did." He entered the Chicago Theological Seminary that fall, and they gave him a church at once—almost an unparalleled thing in that Seminary. It is usually two years or more before students are allowed to preach; but they gave him a church at once, and he had conversions from the very outset. In his middle year at the Seminary a great Pentecost came upon the institution. On the day of prayer for colleges, called by Professor Fisk, the Holy Ghost fell upon us all over the room; and it all came through Ralph Larkin, who took the Holy Spirit by simple faith in God's naked word. Men and women, any one of you may do it tonight, if you are resting in the finished work of Christ. If you are not, you may so rest now. If you have put away all sin, if you simply surrender absolutely to God, if you simply ask for the Holy Ghost and believe that God hears you, you can have Him before you leave the tent.

One more illustration before I close. On July 8, 1894—I shall never forget the day—it was the closing day of the students' conference of the Eastern Universities at Northfield. I had spoken in the church on Sunday morning, and had said nearly the same as I have said to you tonight. I took out my watch, and found that it was precisely twelve o'clock noon. I said, "Young gentlemen, Mr. Moody has invited us to go on the mountain at three o'clock, to wait upon God for the outpouring of the Holy Spirit. It is now precisely twelve o'clock. There are three hours to three o'clock. Some of you cannot wait three hours, neither do you need to do so. Go to your home, to your tent, to your hotel, go out into the woods, go anywhere, and have it out, right now." Three o'clock came, and we gathered up in front of Mr. Moody's mother's house (she was then living), 456 of us —college men, and a few others. Paul Moody counted us, as we passed through the gate and commenced to go up the mountainside. When we had gone part of the way, Mr. Moody said, "I think this is far enough, let us sit down. Young men, have you anything you wish to say, before we pray?" One after another arose, about seventy-five of them, and said something like this: "Mr. Moody, I could not wait till three o'clock. I have been alone with God, and I have received the Holy Ghost." Then Mr. Moody said, when the testimonies were done, "Friends, I cannot see any reason why we, here today, should not kneel right down now, and ask God that the Holy Spirit may fall upon us, as definitely as He fell upon the apostles at Pentecost. Let us pray." We knelt, some of us lay on our faces on the pine-needles. As we had gone up the mountain-side, a big rain-cloud had been gathered overhead; and, just as we began to pray, that rain-cloud broke, and the rain-drops commenced to fall through the over-hanging pine-needles. Another cloud, big with mercy, had been gathering over Northfield for ten days; and, as we prayed, our prayers seemed to penetrate that cloud, and the Holy Ghost fell upon us.

Beloved friends, if I am any judge, a cloud, rich and big with mercy, has been gathering over these tents in Keswick, the last four days. I cannot see why we should not penetrate it with our prayers, right now.

Now, before I pray, I want to ask you something. I want to ask every man and woman, young or old, in the tent, who can honestly say from the heart, "I have accepted Jesus as my Saviour; I am resting entirely in His finished work as the only ground of my acceptance before God. I have put away (or I will now put away, God helping me) everything that God shows me is displeasing to Him. I will surrender absolutely to God, to be wholly His; to go, in His strength, wherever He bids me go, to do whatever He bids me do, to be whatever He would have me to be. I hold nothing back, I give myself absolutely and for ever to God"—if you have done it already, it is just as well, or better. "I believe there is such a thing as a definite gift of the Holy Spirit for me; I want it now, at any cost; and I am ready, God helping me, to put out the simple hand of faith and take it." Or if you have already received the Holy Spirit, as many of you have and desire a new filling tonight, you can stand up. Now, friends —all of you who can say that, honestly—I am going to ask you to rise. But, I beseech you, do not rise unless you mean it from your heart. Don't stand up because somebody else expects you to stand up. Nobody is going to judge you, if you do not rise. Perhaps those who do not rise, are the best people here. I do not see my way to rise upon every invitation given to me in a meeting. If you are not clear, and if you do not mean it, do not rise, I beseech you; we shall not judge you, if you do not. Let me repeat: everyone who can say honestly, "I have accepted Jesus Christ as my Saviour; I am resting entirely in His finished work, as the only ground of my acceptance before God. I have put away (or I will put away out of my life) every known sin, everything that God shows me to be displeasing in His sight. I will surrender, or I have surrendered, all to God, to be utterly and for ever His. I believe there is such a thing for me as the gift of the Holy Spirit, or the baptism of the Spirit"—call it what you please—"and I want it tonight at any cost": all that can honestly say that, rise and remain standing while I pray. And, friends, while these are standing, if there is any unsaved man or woman in the tent, who wants to take the Lord Jesus tonight, you stand, too.

DELIVERANCE FROM THE LAW OF SIN

EVAN H. HOPKINS spoke at the Oxford conference of 1874, which led to the establishment of the Keswick Convention. Rev. Hopkins was perhaps the most outstanding personality behind the scenes in the early years of Keswick. He is often called the "theologian of Keswick," because he more than any other person defined its destinctive message.

DELIVERANCE FROM THE LAW OF SIN

Rev. Evan H. Hopkins

*For to will is present with me; but how to perform that which is
good I find not—*ROMANS 7: 18.

THERE are very many who find great difficulty in the seventh
chapter of Romans, not because that chapter does not re-
echo their own inner experience, but because they find it
impossible to reconcile that experience with a life of victory over
sin. A key, therefore, is needed to explain that difficulty. Practically, we know that too often this seventh chapter of Romans
has been used as a refuge by those who are leading an inconsistent
life; and our spiritual enemy would lead us to use this passage as
a warrant for *expecting defeat*. Is it not true that too often it has been
used, shall I say, as an excuse for sinning? At all events, many of
God's children have come to this chapter for comfort and encouragement while pursuing a course of failure. Surely this was not
the purpose of the apostle in writing the passage. When we come
rightly to understand it, we shall find that this precious portion
of God's Word is full of encouragement, not to those who regard
defeat as inevitable, but to those who believe there is a way of
deliverance, and would know the secret of overcoming sin.

Now, there have been those who, in reading this chapter, have
looked at the passage as describing the experience of an *unconverted*
man. It is very important that we should, at the outset, clearly
understand the spiritual standpoint of the man who utters these
words. If we look at it as the experience of an unconverted man
there arises this difficulty: we have to assume that the apostle,
after having led us on step by step, in the preceding chapters, to
glorious heights of triumph, and fellowship with Christ, suddenly
goes back to the most elementary truths. There would then be no
natural sequence in the line of progress in these chapters. Nor
indeed is this necessary. We shall take the passage as true of the
child of God.

My first point, then, is that the passage is *descriptive of the Christian
man*. The apostle is speaking of himself as a disciple of Jesus Christ.
He *recognises the excellency of God's law*. It is true that a Jew also
would be ready to recognise this: but the apostle uses terms here

in connection with that law which no mere Jew, as such, could have used. His words are strong and emphatic. He says more than any mere Jew could have said: "Wherefore the law is holy, and the commandment holy, and just, and good" (v. 12). Again, "we know that the law is spiritual" (v. 14). He no longer occupies the standpoint of a Jew, because he is not now seeking to be justified by that law. It is by that law that he has been convinced of sin, as we see from the verses which precede our text. It is that law which has pierced him through and through. He has seen the spirituality of that law, and it has dealt a death-blow to all his hopes of salvation by the righteousness of that law. I say that only a man who had been spiritually enlightened could have spoken thus of God's law.

But again, he finds an *inward joy in the requirements of God's law.* Look at verse 22, "For I delight in the law of God after the inward man." That expression is remarkable. It is a strong one. It implies a *sympathetic relationship* between his inmost being and God's law. It indicates an inward harmony with God's commandments. Now, the natural man could never have said this, and the sinner, however deeply awakened, could never have used such language; he could not have truthfully said that he rejoiced in the requirements of God's law, after the inward man—and by the inward man, I take it, we must understand that part of his being which had been born from above. The language, therefore, is the language of a Christian man, of a converted man.

Then, notice again that his *desires and intentions are on the side of the law.* The law is "good." "To will is present with me"—to will the good, to do the good—"but how to perform that which is good, I find not." This cannot be asserted of any soul that has been untouched by divine grace. I say that we have here the description of a Christian man. But a Christian man *regarded in himself,* apart from faith in Christ. "But how can such a condition be possible?" You say, "It is utterly inconceivable."

Well, let us come to the point by considering what is meant by the expression, "in Christ." It is a favourite expression of the apostle Paul. The germ of that expression we have in John 15. What do we understand by our blessed Lord's words when He says in that chapter, "Without me ye can do nothing"? The *standing* of every believer is "in Christ," without any exception. You are accepted "in Christ." God looks at you "in Christ." But there is another aspect; there is another "in Christ," not simply the "in Christ" of *position* or standing, but the "in Christ" of *condition,* or fellowship. There is such a thing as not abiding "in Christ." There is such a thing as being out of communion—out of Christ in that sense. I believe it is to this condition that our

Lord referred when He said, "Without me"—apart from me, outside of me—"ye can do nothing."

And so, in the passage before us, what is it that we have in these twelve verses, 14–25? The passage is a parenthesis in the line of argument, and for a moment the apostle is contemplating himself as a converted man, and yet as apart from Christ. His desire is heavenwards; his will is on the right side, but he lacks the adequate *power* to perform; sin is stronger than the strength of his will, stronger than all his holy tendencies upward, which he has by virtue of his new birth. And if he lacks power, what then? There is failure, fruitless struggle, painful effort, continuous conflict and defeat. "I see not only the law of my mind, which delights in God's requirement. I see another law in my members, warring against the law of my mind, and bringing me into captivity to the law of sin which is in my members" (v. 23). "To will the good is present with me, but the evil is also present, and how to perform that which is good I find not."

Now, I believe there are multitudes of Christians who are practically in that condition. But you say, "Does not the apostle describe here his own present experience?" Not necessarily. "But he is not using the past tense; he is using the present tense." Yes, but he is not speaking from the standpoint of a present *experience*, though I believe he is speaking from the standpoint of a present *conviction* as to the tendency of the two laws. Therefore he uses the present tense. For instance, when I say, "Fire burns me," I do not mean precisely the same thing as when I say, "The fire is burning me." In the first case I am simply describing the property of fire; in the second I am giving a description of the present action of fire within the sphere of my consciousness. But still I use the present tense. And so the apostle, as one has said, is giving us here a "diagram" of the condition of things apart from the divine remedy. As if he said, Look for a moment at what you are as a converted man, as a renewed soul, as a Christian, as a child of God. You have the summing up of the matter in the last verse of the chapter. "So then, with the mind *I myself* serve the law of God, but with the flesh the law of sin." The "I myself-life" is one thing, but the "Christ-life" is another. There are multitudes of Christians who are living the "I myself-life." They know what pardon is; they know what it is to come to the Fountain; they know what it is to look to Jesus Christ in times of difficulty and perplexity, and to come back again to Him with their guilt, and get forgiven; but they are living the "I myself-life" instead of the "Christ-life."

Now let us turn to *God's remedy*. In order to be able to apply a remedy you must, like the physician, make a true diagnosis of the disease from which the patient is suffering. Now I find in the fifth, sixth, and seventh chapters of Romans three distinct aspects of sin; and in order that we may see what is God's threefold provision, we must understand the nature of sin in this threefold aspect.

Look at chapter 5. There we see sin as a load of guilt—sin *upon* us. Come to chapter 6, and there we see sin as a master—sin *over* us. Then in chapter 7, sin as a law—*within* us. As the Lord Jesus Christ is God's remedy, we must see the corresponding aspects of that remedy as meeting these various aspects of sin. We have three little prepositions of deep meaning. The keynote of the fifth chapter is, "Christ died *for* the ungodly" (Rom. 5: 6); of the sixth chapter, "I died *with* Christ" (6: 6); and of the seventh and eighth chapters, "*in* Christ." In order that I may know deliverance from sin, as the burden of guilt, I must see that He died *for* me. That is *substitution*. Every Christian knows what substitution means, and some of us, who have grasped that thought, fancied we had grasped the whole of the Gospel as if there was nothing more to know.

But the Spirit of God leads on in the next chapter, to see another aspect of Christ. Not only has Christ died for me, and the guilt been taken away, but I have to see that I died *with* Christ—and *with* expresses *identification*. When we grasp the truth contained in that thought, we understand what it is to be delivered from sin as a master. And when we have got as far as that, we fancy, some of us, that we have got it all. No. We are still troubled and cast down, because we have not been brought to see the secret of deliverance from *sin as a law* in us. But now we are brought to understand God's remedy in the meaning of that little word "in." To be "in Christ" is *not only union, but fellowship*.

You have noticed, have you not, that in those eleven verses to which I have referred as a parenthesis, more than thirty times does the apostle allude to himself in one form or other. Not once does he refer to God the Father, the Son, or the Holy Spirit. The reason is that he is regarding himself as a Christian apart for the moment from the remedy; and he says that in spite of all our good intentions and earnestness, and our will being on the right side, the law of sin is too strong for us.

I have illustrated the point sometimes in this way. Suppose that I take a rod and attach to it a piece of lead. I drop it into a tank of water. By the law of sinking bodies, it descends; that illustrates the law of sin. Now I get a piece of cork, and fasten that also to the rod, and placing it in the water I see that by the law of floating bodies, it has a tendency to ascend. But the lifting power of the cork is not strong enough to overcome the downward tendency of the lead, so that it may be kept from sinking. It rises and sinks alternately. There you have the "up and down" life. "I myself" by the cork serving the law of floating bodies, and "I myself" by the lead obeying the law of sinking bodies. "Up and down."

Now turn to 8: 2 and we read, "For the law of the Spirit of life in Christ Jesus *hath made me free from the law of sin and death.*" What has taken place? Let us suppose that I place my rod with the lead and the cork into a little life-belt, and I put them into the tank of water. The rod now does not sink. Why? Because it is in the life-belt. There is sufficient lifting-power in it to keep it from sinking; but it is only as it is in the life-belt that it has the benefit of that law. It is the power of a superior law counteracting the other law. The lead is not taken away, but the rod has the benefit of a stronger power so long as it abides in the life-belt.

A working man to whom I used this illustration at once grasped the principle, and in prayer afterwards he said, "O God, we thank Thee for the life-belt, we thank Thee for the Lord Jesus Christ, who is the life-belt. We thank Thee we cannot sink so long as we abide in the life-belt; but may we never forget, O Lord, that while we are floating inside the life-belt, that the lead is there all the same."

Here, then, are the main points to be borne in mind. Sin is a load of guilt, but Christ died *for* me; sin is a master, but I died *with* Christ; sin is a law, but by abiding *in* Christ I am made "*free* from the law of sin and death." It is not an attainment, you see. It is not something that has taken place in you, so that you no longer have the tendency to sin. That is not it at all. The law of gravitation is not suspended when, instead of sinking, you float on the water within the life-belt; but it is *counteracted by a superior law*, and this is "the law of the Spirit of life in Christ Jesus."

It is thus that I read Romans 7. We do not triumph by virtue of our own struggles and efforts to keep ourselves from sinking, but by abiding in the life-belt and letting Christ have the whole weight of our load, which He counteracts by His superior power. Oh, to know the secret of this *abiding*! That is what we have to learn. Let us begin to learn it now. Hence we see we must not only know what it is to be in Christ in the sense of standing for our acceptance and justification, but also in the sense of *abiding*, that is, of fellowship with Him, if we would live in the power of His victorious life.

CRISIS AND PROCESS

EVAN H. HOPKINS has been called the "theologian of Keswick." He became editor of Keswick's official periodical, *The Christian's Pathway of Power,* in 1875. This monthly journal was renamed *The Life of Faith* in 1879.

CRISIS AND PROCESS

Rev. Evan H. Hopkins

Our subject is: "A crisis with a view to a process." There are few things connected with the Keswick movement which have so much puzzled people as the apparent contradiction, that the blessing is both instantaneous and progressive. Those who have been brought into definite blessing, along the line of sanctification by faith, have borne witness to the fact that they had been brought into an experience of what the Lord Jesus Christ can be to them for holiness, with a suddenness that has been as striking as the change has been blessed and soul-satisfying. The sense of rest, the sense of all-sufficiency of grace in Christ, has come to them with a wonderful instantaneousness. But this has been followed by an experience of its progressiveness that they never knew before. Sanctification in the sense of conformity to the life and character of Christ is a process, a gradual process, a continuous process, an endless process. But sanctification, in the sense of a definite decision for holiness, a thorough and whole-hearted dedication to God, the committal of the whole being to Him, is a crisis; and the crisis must take place before we really know the process. Before you can draw a line you must begin with a point. The line is the process, the point is the crisis. Have you come to the point? Have you come to the point that you are decided to-day, now, here, that you will be holy? Or, are you only earnestly praying that God will enable you to come to the point? Some people have been doing that for years. Do you see the difference?

Two men were arguing upon this subject. One had been brought to understand it not only theoretically but practically, experimentally, and the other one was fairly puzzled—he could not see it. The first man said, "How did you come from London to Keswick?" "I came by train." "Was it by one sudden jump into Keswick?" "Oh, no, I came along more and more." "Yes, I see; but first you got into the train. How did you get into the carriage? Was it more and more?" "No, I just stepped in." "Exactly: that was the crisis; and as you journeyed along, it was more and more. There is the crisis; there is the process."

I want to show you different passages of Scripture, and to

61

indicate where we have the crisis, and where we have the process.
We will begin with *the crisis*, and we will take, first, the act of (i)
separation from all defilement. Will you turn to 2 Corinthians 7: 1?
We have in that verse an act of separation from all defilement.
"Having therefore these promises, dearly beloved, let us cleanse
ourselves from all defilement of the flesh and spirit." Look at that
act. Is it to be done gradually by degrees, or instantaneously?
The tense shows us that it is definite and decisive. There is the
crisis. God has given you light; the light has shone into your heart.
You are conscious of defilement. How will you deal with it?
God says, "Cleanse yourselves"—a decisive act of separation
from all that you know to be evil. There is the crisis.

Then there is the act of (ii) *putting off evil habits.* Ephesians 4: 31
—of course there are many other passages; I am only giving you
a few—"Let all bitterness, and wrath, and anger, and clamour,
and evil speaking, be put away from you, with all malice." It
does not mean that you are to be a *little less* censorious to-day
than you were yesterday. The force of the exhortation is that
you put it off, as you put off a coat, so that you are separate from
it. Here in this passage we have a list of evil habits. Remember
we were not born into the world with evil habits. The evil nature
is one thing; the evil habit is another. There we have, then, a
crisis—how we are to deal with evil habits.

Take, again, the act of (iii) *"laying aside every weight"* (Heb.
12: 1). Are there any weights in your life impeding your progress,
marring your influence? How are you to deal with them? Shall
we pray about them? Well, that is good; but praying of itself
is not enough. God says, "Lay them aside." How shall we lay
them aside? Very gradually, by degrees? Not, if we obey the
word that we have before us, remembering the force of the
tense. If you have a weight, you know what it is to drop it. That
is not a gradual act, but a decisive, definite act. Are there any
weights in your life about which God has a controversy with
you? Now here is the point. God has brought us up here for
this purpose, that we should deal definitely with these things.
The act of laying aside is a definite act—not a process, but a
crisis.

Further, there is the act of (iv) *handing our bodies over to God.* We
little realise that while the spirit and soul are right with God,
we may still keep the body in our own hands. I suppose the body
is the last thing that the Christian really gives over to God.
His gifts, his possessions? Yes. Spirit and soul? Yes. The body?
Well, we have not done with it; it is useful, we think, we want
to use it for ourselves. Romans 12: 1, "Present your *bodies* . . ."
That is what we have to bring. Take the words just as they stand.

You are a Christian; the Holy Spirit has touched your spirit, you have eternal life. The citadel of our being is the spirit, the city the soul, and the walls of the city are the body. The five senses, the five gates, are in the walls, and the evil one gets through the gates. You cannot keep the body, you cannot keep the walls. "Except the Lord keep the city, the watchman waketh but in vain." Therefore, "present your bodies," hand them right over into God's hand—a definite, not a gradual act. There is a crisis; the tense in the original points clearly to that. What you have been trying to do gradually God wants you to do suddenly, immediately, up to the light you have.

Then, take the act of (v) *being divinely adjusted*. Hebrews 13: 20, 21, "The God of peace . . . make you perfect in every good work to do His will." Here is God's act. He makes you perfect. What is the meaning? He adjusts you; you are in a state of spiritual dislocation, you are out of joint, and the prayer is that God should put you into joint. He does not do it gradually; it is done instantaneously. This is what has taken place in the case of hundreds of souls in this very tent. In a few brief moments the whole inner being has been adjusted. First, spiritual adjustment, and afterwards spiritual enduement. There we have again the tense that points to an immediate decisive act, God's act. When we present ourselves to Him, when we yield our whole being to Him and lay ourselves at His feet, then He takes us and puts us into joint, He adjusts us, He brings us into harmony. What we have been trying to do gradually, all our life, now that we hand ourselves over to Him, He does immediately. After those words in Hebrews which I have just quoted, we have "working in you." There is the part that is progressive. Or, again, "to do His will." Doing His will is the progressive part. Being put into joint, being made perfect, adjusted, is the crisis.

Take another passage. There is the act of being (vi) *divinely appropriated*, or wholly sanctified. 1 Thessalonians 5: 23, "The very God of peace sanctify you wholly," that is, sanctify not your spirit and soul only, but body also: the whole man, spirit, soul and body. Sanctification on our side is giving ourselves to God. Sanctification on God's side is appropriating us unto Himself. That is the positive side of sanctification, when God Himself, the Holy One, takes possession of us, appropriates us to Himself. Here is God's act, and the remarkable thing is that it is still in the aorist, pointing to a crisis. The blessing that so many people have realised as a sudden blessing—here it is put before us as God's act, and pointing to a crisis.

Take one more text under the head of crisis, and referring, this time to the act of (vii) *enthroning Christ as Lord*. 1 Peter 3: 15,

"Sanctify in your hearts Christ as Lord." (R.V.) We have here a beautiful thought. Your heart is looked at as a sanctuary—not only as a city. Christ is within, and you know Him as Jesus, and you know Him as Christ, but how imperfectly you have known Him as Lord! It is not that a new Person has to enter in, but it is a new revelation of the same Person to your soul. And when you see Him as Lord, you enthrone Him. To sanctify Christ as Lord is to enthrone Him in your heart. He who is on the throne in glory is now to be on the throne in your heart. That is not a gradual process. The tense here points to a decisive act. It is a crisis. Is not that wonderful? I want you to bear it in mind. So that we not only look at the verb, but at the tense, and this shows us the duty of immediate response, immediate obedience.

What have we seen? That separation from all defilement is an immediate act; that the putting off of evil habits is an immediate act; that laying aside every weight is an immediate act; that handing over our bodies to God is a definite immediate act; that being divinely adjusted is a divine act, and God does it at once, immediately; that being divinely appropriated, or wholly sanctified, is God's act, an immediate act; that enthroning Christ in our hearts as Lord is an immediate act, the act of a moment. All those passages that I have quoted point to a crisis.

Shall we turn now to *the process?*

(i) *Spiritual conformity.* 2 Corinthians 3: 18, "But we all, with unveiled face beholding," or reflecting "as a mirror the glory of the Lord, are changed." Here is the present tense, here is the process, gradual, continuous, endless. This is what you perfectly understand. And the process follows the crisis. "From glory to glory." There is the growth, the advancement, the process.

Take another. (ii) *Spiritual renewal.* 2 Corinthians 4: 16, "The inward man is renewed day by day," is being renewed. That is progressive.

(iii) *Spiritual strengthening.* Colossians 1: 11, "Strengthened with all might, according to the power of His glory." That is Christ on the throne. "The riches of His grace" is Christ on the cross; "the riches of His glory" is Christ on the throne. From the throne came the gift of the Spirit, a stream perpetually flowing. "Being strengthened." There is the process. You do not get the power put into your hands that you may use it independently of Him; it is always in the Lord's hand, and it is always flowing from the throne. "Being strengthened with all might." Are you in the stream? A perpetual reception. There is the process.

(iv) *Progressive purity.* There is such a thing as an instantaneous cleansing. But, remember, there is the other side of the truth—progressive purity. 1 John 3: 3, "Every man that hath this hope in Him," that is, in Christ, "purifieth," is purifying, "himself, even as He is pure." An endless process.

(v) *Spiritual growth.* 2 Peter 3: 18, "Grow in grace." I need not dwell upon the fact that all growth, of necessity, is progressive.

(vi) *Progressive sanctification.* Hebrews 10: 14, "For by one offering He hath perfected for ever them that are sanctified," or "are being sanctified."

Lastly (vii) *transformation of character.* Romans 12: 1, 2, "I beseech you . . . that ye present your bodies . . . And be ye transformed by the renewing of your mind." We have both here put together. The crisis, "present"; the process, "Be ye transformed." How closely they are connected there! I have given you, then, the crisis and the process, and, I trust—I am speaking especially to my younger hearers—you have marked these places in your Bibles to distinguish between the one and the other.

Now we come to the practical question: *Is the crisis to be repeated?* If I have once consecrated myself to God, am I not to consecrate myself to Him again? My answer to that question is this. Take, for instance, the act of consecration. Is it to be done over and over again? or is it done once for all? I say, Yes, it is to be done again *in the sense of restoration.* You have slipped back, your attitude of consecration has not been maintained; you have to come back again, you have to repeat the act undoubtedly.

But, I say again, Yes, it has to be repeated *in the sense of confirmation.* You consecrated yourself to God yesterday; you did it thoroughly, honestly; you wholly gave yourself to Him. You woke up this morning, and what was the attitude you took, if you took the right attitude? Just one of confirmation. I did that act yesterday, and I say "Amen" to the act this morning, not because I have to do it over again, as if I had never done it before; and yet I do do it as an act of confirmation.

Let me close with one little illustration. A beautiful copy of *Aesop's Fables* was presented to a certain family that I know, and that book was very much used in the nursery. After many years, when the children had grown up, you can imagine that the leaves got loose and scattered, as the book had been a good deal pulled about. An artist called at that house, and his eye was attracted by the beauty of the illustrations. He saw that they had been done by a man who knew how to draw. He asked the head of the household, "Would you have any objection to giving me that book? I should prize it much." The head of the family took the book and gathered up all the stray leaves, and put them all together, and taking the book in his hand, he said to his friend, "You are welcome to the book; it is yours. I give to you." The artist took away the book.

Two or three days afterwards one or two more stray leaves were discovered. What did the head of the family say? Did he say, "Dear me! I never gave that book thoroughly to my friend after all! I suppose I must have him back and go over the whole process again; I must tell him that now I give him the book afresh because I did not give it wholly to him yesterday"? No; he says, "I gave the book to my friend, and the *whole* book; therefore, I will pass these leaves on to him; they do not belong to me." There was a fresh discovery, but he remembered that he gave the whole book, and those leaves were all included in the gift, and so he passed them on to his friend.

Do you see how that applies? When you consecrated yourself to God, you gave the whole book, so far as you knew. But, as the Spirit has been leading you on to make fresh discoveries, what are you to do? The devil says, "That was not a genuine act of consecration; you must do it all over again." But you say, "No; I knew I could never do anything perfectly, but I can do it up to the light that God gives me. I can do that thoroughly. In that sense I did give myself wholly to the Lord yesterday, or last week, and now I discover fresh things, and pass them on at once, immediately." In that sense the crisis is repeated—but it is an act of confirmation. See that, every morning, and every day, and many times during the day, you can say "Amen" to the fact that you have handed yourself wholly to Him. In that sense it is repeated, and you need not backslide in order to do it over again.

THE FULLNESS
OF THE SPIRIT

CHARLES INWOOD was pastor of a Methodist congregation in Belfast, Ireland, before becoming a full-time
evangelist for the Keswick Convention. He first preached at
Keswick in 1892.

THE FULLNESS OF THE SPIRIT

Rev. Dr. Charles Inwood

And Ananias went his way, and entered into the house; and putting his hands on him said, Brother Saul, the Lord, even Jesus, that appeared unto thee in the way as thou camest, hath sent me, that thou mightest receive thy sight, and be filled with the Holy Ghost —Acts 9: 17.

I WANT to put before you, in the simplest possible form, some of the teaching of the Word of God respecting the fullness of the Holy Spirit. I long that, here and now, there may fall upon our minds and hearts the mighty, resistless power of Pentecost, so that our life may never again be what, till now, it has been. I would not forget, nor have you forgotten, our utter dependence upon the Holy Spirit. We are dependent upon the Holy Spirit for all our experimental knowledge of the Lord Jesus as Saviour, and Master, and Lord, and indwelling life. In the nature of things there can be no antagonism between God the Son and God the Holy Ghost. We have no more of the indwelling Christ than we have of the indwelling Spirit. We are not fully mastered or possessed by Jesus until we are mastered and possessed by God the Holy Ghost.

Let us then, first of all, point out the simple teaching of this portion of Scripture as to the possibility of being filled with the Spirit; and then we will speak of those simple conditions upon which this fullness may be ours here and now.

There are four elementary truths taught in this text. First, *It is possible for us to be filled with the Spirit.* Second, *It is possible to be filled with the Spirit upon the threshold of the new life*; next, *It is possible to be filled suddenly*; and then, *It is possible to know it.*

First, *It is possible to be filled with the Spirit.* Oh, how easy it is to utter a sentence like that, but what a solemn, glorious possibility is expressed by those words—to be full of the Spirit as the tree in springtime is full of sap: full from the deepest root, full in the trunk, full in the branches, full in the stem, full in the twigs, full in the leaf, full from the lowest root right away to the farthermost leaf; full as the human body of a healthy person is full of life; full as the white-hot iron is full of the fire! You take the iron cold and dark, you put it into the fire, and the fire enters into it, and soon the fire changes its colour and its power; and now that white-hot iron is possessed, inter-penetrated by the fire within it, and so full is that iron of the fire that if you touch the iron you feel, not so much the iron, but the fire which possesses the iron.

And it is possible to be so full of the Spirit that all bondage, and all friction, and all the fever of lust disappear; so full of the Spirit that selfishness in motive, in intention, in purpose, in endeavour disappears; so full of the Spirit that all open and secret sympathy with sin disappears; so full of the Spirit that all conscious and wilful resistance to God disappears; so full that God becomes present, predominant, supreme, throughout the length and breadth of one's whole being; so full that God becomes the supreme law in the soul, God becomes the supreme authority in the soul, and God becomes the supreme power in the soul; and as a result there is complete subjection of the heart and life to the purpose and the will of God. If one had no other evangel for God's people, one would gladly go round the world to make known a glorious possibility like that. It is possible for you with your environment, you with your past, you with the forbidding future; you where you live, man, woman, it is possible for you here and now to be filled with the Holy Ghost.

Then, *It is possible to be filled with the Spirit on the threshold of the new life.* Saul had only three days before he received that wonderful vision which completely changed him. The Samaritan believers had only recently received the Lord Jesus, when they received the Spirit in fullness. And to me it is an intensely precious truth that the youngest believer, the one who most recently received the Lord Jesus, may here and now receive the wondrous fullness of the Holy Ghost.

Some years ago, away in America, there was a young lad, wild and thoughtless and reckless; one who attended the different churches in the town where he lived, only to make fun of all he saw and heard; one who, as the result, became such a public nuisance that the pastors of the churches deliberately refused to let him come any longer inside the sanctuaries. This lad heard one day of a great camp-meeting which was to be held some miles away from where he lived. He had no idea as to what a camp-meeting was, but he thought he would go and see what it was like. So on the Sunday when the camp-meeting opened, that young lad was present, present at all the services during the day, and made fun of the novelty of the services, and the methods adopted; and he left the Sunday night service altogether untouched by anything he had seen or heard. Yet he thought he would like to go back again; so during the week he drove away from his home to where the camp-meeting was being held, and he stayed for the services that day. He was present at the night service, and during the address God the Holy Spirit sent the shaft of conviction into his mind and heart. The minister in charge of the camp-meeting said that if there were any people present who desired to give their hearts to Jesus, they might come forward to what was called "the altar," and the first person in that large congregation to come forward was this thoughtless, wild, reckless lad. Near to where he sat there was a saint, a dear old woman, who knew something of the boy; and when she saw him come forward, she stepped out of her seat, and came forward with him. He came up to what was a stump of an old tree—for the camp-ground was away in the forest—and there he knelt, and she beside him; and there God the Holy Spirit presented to him his sin, and broke him down with an utter and overwhelming sense of guilt and shame. There he knelt and prayed, and there she knelt beside him, and prayed with him. The hours went by, and other seekers came forward, and found the Lord Jesus Christ, and went away rejoicing in Him; and this lad was still there praying, crying, longing for the salvation of the Lord Jesus. There beside him knelt that dear old woman, who was determined to wait with him and pray with him until he did receive salvation; and between eleven and twelve o'clock at night, when they two were the only persons in the tent, that poor fellow rolled the burden of his guilt over on the Lord Jesus, and God for Christ's sake pardoned his sins, and gave him the conscious joy of pardoning love. He rose from his knees rejoicing in Jesus as his Saviour, his face all luminous with the new joy he had found in the Lord Jesus.

Then this dear saint said to him: "Joseph, will you come with me to my lodgings; I have a little book there, *Counsels for Young Converts*, and if you will only take it and read it prayerfully, I believe it will be a real help to you." In the darkness they wandered from the camp-ground to where she was lodging, and in the darkness she went up into her room to lay her hand on this book, and to bring it to Joseph, who was waiting outside. All unknown to her, by accident, as men would say, but by the guidance of God, she laid her hand upon another book. She came down in the darkness, not knowing that she had brought another book —which she gave to him, telling him to go home and read it. When he reached home, and began reading it, he found, of course, that it was not the book, *Counsels for Young Converts*, but it was a book on the very subject that we are dealing with here, in this

Convention—cleansing from sin, and the indwelling of the Holy Spirit in the heart of the believer. He did not go off to bed, but he sat up reading, and as he read, even in the joy of his conscious love to Jesus, he became convicted of the fact that there was a fullness of the Holy Spirit possible in Jesus Christ even for him; and there, alone in his room, with that book, and with God, he was led to see his need of this mighty baptism of the Spirit, and to trust as simply and definitely for the fullness of the Spirit as a few hours before he had trusted for the pardon of his sins. And the same God who gave him pardon when he trusted, kneeling at that old stump in the camp-ground, flooded the soul of that young believer with the overflowing fullness of God the Holy Spirit, and from that day till today that young man has been, and is now, a faithful, honoured servant of the Lord Jesus Christ. He has been used of God in the salvation of thousands of souls, and the sanctification of large numbers of believers; and that glorious fullness of the Spirit was given to that young heart consciously, within a few hours of the time when he trusted in Jesus for the pardon of his sins.

If there be one young Christian here to whom Satan is making this suggestion: "There is such a blessing as the fullness of the Spirit, but you must go on two, five, ten years, and become a mature Christian before it may be yours," I tell you in the name of my Master that if you are a child of God by faith in Jesus, if you have been born again of God the Holy Ghost, then here and now, though you be the very youngest believer, God is willing to fill you with the Spirit.

Again, *It is possible to be filled with the Spirit suddenly*, as this verse here teaches.

One does not desire, even unintentionally, to dogmatise on so sacred a theme as this, but I would like to call your attention to this fact—that all through the Acts of the Apostles you come into contact with cases of sudden filling of the Holy Spirit. There is not one single case in the Acts of the Apostles recorded which was not a case of sudden filling. It was *suddenly* on the day of Pentecost, it was *suddenly* in the 4th chapter, *suddenly* with the Samaritan believers, *suddenly* with Saul, *suddenly* with the Gentiles in the house of Cornelius, *suddenly* with the Ephesian believers. They went in many cases into a meeting, not filled with the Spirit; and before they left the meeting, a prayer-meeting in some instances, they were filled with the Holy Ghost.

It is our joy to tell unconverted people that they do not need to wait one single hour for the salvation of the Lord Jesus. We rejoice to tell them, when they come into our services, that though they came in strangers and aliens from the commonwealth of

Israel, the Lord Jesus Christ is able to save them and change them before they go home. We praise God for the privilege of telling of a present and immediate salvation for all who need it. But it is equally true, and equally our joy, to tell you that, if there are in this tent a thousand saved souls who till now have not been filled with the Spirit, my God in His grace and power and mercy can fill every heart in that thousand now. You came to the meeting a stranger to this fullness; you need not go away without being filled with God the Holy Ghost.

There is one thought more in this connection: *It is possible to know that we are filled with the Spirit.*

How? Not by inference merely, not by the fruits which may follow merely, not by a new sense of peace, or a new sense of power, or a new sense of joy, though that may all come; but beyond all else by a new, overwhelming sense of God, the consciousness, the awful and yet glorious consciousness, that God is at last in actual and undisputed possession of the whole temple of one's being.

Yes, it is possible, and yet, before I deal with the conditions, let me remind you that the consciousness of the Spirit's indwelling and infilling is not equally vivid in all Christian hearts. Therefore you must not judge yourself by the vivid consciousness which may be given to another.

Further, the consciousness of the Spirit's indwelling is not always equally vivid in the same surrendered and obedient heart. I pray you, remember these two simple statements, for they will save you from much trouble in the temptations which will assail you when the Convention is over and gone.

But now, having laid this very simple foundation, I want to deal next with the *conditions* upon which this present fullness of the Holy Spirit may become yours. I want to remind you at once that this is a question between your heart and God. No matter how many people are in this tent, each one must now get alone with God, if we are to receive this fullness of the Spirit. And so, as I deal with the three conditions, God helping me, I will put them in a form in which each thirsting, hungering soul may express its need to God here and now.

The three conditions on which we desire to speak are these: First, *confession*; next, *surrender*; and next, *faith*.

First, *Confession.* If the confession of sin brings a sense of shame to the heart that makes it, the confession which in my Master's name I want you to make honestly now, will bring a sense of shame and humiliation to your heart. Here is the ground which your confession must cover, if that confession is to be such as God demands from you. That confession must cover these four points: First, "O God, I confess with shame and sorrow that I am not filled with Thy Spirit, though I know I may be, and ought to be." The proud, carnal heart in the Christian will rebel against that confession, all the more because you are a Christian, all the more because you are a Christian worker; and still more if you have been a Christian worker and leader for many years. But you will have to make it. "O God, though a minister of the Gospel of Jesus Christ, I am not filled with Thy Spirit." "Though I have been a missionary to the heathen, Lord, I am not filled with Thy Spirit." "Though I am a prominent worker in my church, I am not filled with Thy Spirit." "Though I have known Jesus as my Saviour for ten or twenty years, I am not filled with Thy Spirit." "O God, my heart breaks in Thy presence as I confess to Thee that, though here as a Christian and a worker, I am not filled with the Holy Spirit."

Then the confession will also include this: "O God, it is my own fault that I am not filled." Let me be honest with you. Do not blame your lack of teaching as the real cause. Remember this, if you are saved, you have the life of God in your soul, you have the Word of God in your hand, you have the Spirit of God for your teacher; and with these you have all you need to know. If you had never heard a message on this subject, or never attended a convention, or never read a single address on the subject, you cannot, if that be your condition, take any other ground but this: "O God, if I am not filled with Thy Spirit, the fault really and truly is mine."

Then there is the confession—and that also makes the heart ache: "O God, I see at last I shall never be right till I am filled with Thy Spirit. I shall never have complete victory over tempta-tion till I am filled; I shall never fully realise the Christ-like character until I am filled; I shall never accomplish Thy purpose in redeeming and saving me, until I am filled. O God, I see it now. There is something wrong in my heart, there is something wrong in my service, there is something wrong in my life; and I now see what till now I never saw—it is all because I am not, day by day, filled with God the Holy Ghost."

Then there comes the fourth thought in the confession: "O God, I confess that I want to be filled, cost what it may. It may cost me from one point of view very much; I may be called a 'fanatic,' I may be called 'extreme,' I may be dubbed by the name of 'Keswick,' I may be called a 'perfectionist,' I may lose the goodwill of those who work with me in the church, I may lose even my pastorate if I preach this Gospel; but, O God, at last I see this is for me the question of questions, and at last my heart says, cost what it may, O God, I do want to be filled with the Holy Spirit." To make that four-fold confession frankly, honestly, humbly to God, will bring a keener ache to your heart, and more tears to your eyes, and more burning humiliation before God, than anything else you ever did. At least, some of us have found it so. But the confession must be made if the blessing is to be yours.

Then if you have made, or do now make, the confession, you are ready for the second step; and it is this: "O God, in obedience to Thy command and entreaty, I now yield myself wholly to Thee, that Thou mayest fill me with the Holy Spirit." Now that means something more than giving up everything for the Lord Jesus. It means the one supreme act of *self-surrender* which carries everything else along with it; it means the placing of one's whole being upon the altar, which altar is Jesus Christ the Lord; for the gift that you make of yourself to God will not be acceptable to God, or accepted by God, unless you make it in and through the Lord Jesus Christ. There is no way of access to God for you except through the Lord Jesus Christ, your Saviour and your Redeemer. And so the whole being is placed upon Jesus Christ, who is the altar, in simple, total, unreserved abandonment to God; and that means a good deal, too, as some of us know.

But now the third step: "O God, trusting in Thy faithfulness to Thine own Word, I now dare to believe that the Holy Spirit takes entire possession of me." You draw your breath, and you say: "No, I cannot say that; even to God I cannot say that. I cannot say it, because I do not feel I am filled." No, you cannot feel you are filled in any case until you are filled; but remember —for it is a rock upon which so many seekers seem to stumble— remember that God never gives feeling to enable us to trust Him, God never gives feeling to encourage us to trust Him, God never gives feeling to show that we have really and utterly trusted Him. God only gives feeling when He sees we trust Him apart from all feeling, resting on His own Word, and on His own faithfulness to His promise. Never till then can the feeling possibly come; and God will give the feeling in such measure and at such a time as His love sees best for the individual case.

And now remember this one thought; and it is important. There may be an interval between the moment when you *by faith* claim the Spirit and the moment when you are made conscious of the infilling of the Holy Ghost. It does seem to me as if the time between the moment when we surrender and trust, and the moment when God comes and consciously fills the temple—that interval is the really critical stage, if we are seeking to be filled with the Spirit. That interval may be short or long. I have known some who definitely abandoned themselves, and trusted for the fullness of the Spirit, and the very moment they did it, God so wondrously came in and filled and flooded their souls, that they could not speak under the very burden of the glory of His presence. But I have known others who yielded just as intelligently and just as fully, and trusted just as simply and honestly in God, but did not receive the consciousness of the infilling of the Holy Spirit at the moment they trusted.

May I in all humility be permitted to give a witness; it may help somebody. In my own case, God led me definitely and early one Friday morning, simply as a little child, to trust Him for this priceless gift, the fullness of the Holy Spirit. By simple, naked faith I took the gift, but I was not conscious of receiving anything. All through that day there seemed even a deeper dryness and dullness in one's soul—no new pulsations, no new sense of the presence of God. How often during that day the devil came and said: "You have trusted God to fill you with the Spirit; see how you feel! Why, you do not feel that you have as much of God in you today as last week!" That was true, and Friday went, and Saturday came, and it seemed a very long day; there was the same dryness and the same absence of the sensible presence of God, and during the Saturday the tempter came still more powerfully assailing one's faith in God. But one held on to God, to His promise, to His unchanging faithfulness to His own Word. It is always a thousand times better to trust in the faithfulness of God than in the fitfulness of one's poor senses. Sunday came. Sunday morning just as dry as ever; and the Sunday morning service came, and during that Sunday morning service, during the proclamation of the message—for, praise God, He can bless the soul of the speaker even while speaking the message in the Master's name; if He did not, I do not know what some of us would do—but that morning, as one was speaking His message to the people, there came silently stealing into one's heart a strange, new sense of ease and rest and peace. That is how it began and then it deepened, hour by hour, during the day, deepened in the service in the evening, and in the after-meeting it seemed to culminate in one great tidal wave of the story of God that swelled, and submerged, and inter-penetrated, and broke one down in silent, holy adoration in God's presence. God had fulfilled His promise on the Friday morning, but He wanted to test the soul of His servant, and God sent that sweet, sacred, never-to-be-forgotten sense of His presence at the earliest moment that it was good for His yielded, obedient, trusting child.

And some of you may with all your heart yield tonight and trust tonight, as simply as you trusted the Lord Jesus Christ for the pardon of your sins long ago; and there may be no change in your consciousness here tonight. Remember, that period is, as I have said, a critical period. Many Christians yield, as I trust many of you will, and simply as a little child trust for the fullness of the Holy Spirit, and there is no change at the time, and then they begin to look into their hearts and begin to say—and the tempter is always near to give the suggestion—"Ah, I wonder was I deluded last night? I wonder is it a mistake? I wonder was it a little bit of fanaticism? I wonder whether, after all, I am filled with the Spirit; I do not feel I am filled, I wonder if I am." And then a step further: "I am afraid I am not!" Then a step further: "I am sure I am not!" And there, without knowing it, they slip right down from the position of simple, whole-hearted trust in the faithfulness of God, to positive unbelief.

How is that interval, long or short, to be occupied? Not by wondering, not by fearing, not by doubting whether the Spirit has entered, but by simple, persistent, resolute, triumphant belief that God is faithful to you, and keeps His word here and now. It must come to that.

Now, beloved, my message is done. This fullness of the Spirit is for every saved soul in this great congregation, and if here and now you fulfil the conditions, the Lord will come to His temple, even the Messenger of the covenant; He will come, and your heart, your being, your life will become inter-penetrated, filled, conquered, mastered by the presence of the Almighty Holy Ghost. May God make this a Pentecost, a definite, real, drastic, revolutionising Pentecost to our waiting hearts.

ADEQUACY FOR LIFE AND WITNESS

PAUL S. REES, a minister of the Evangelical Covenant Church, edited *World Vision* magazine (1964–72) and has been a long-time contributor to *Eternity, Christianity Today,* and other evangelical periodicals.

ADEQUACY FOR LIFE AND WITNESS

Rev. Dr. Paul S. Rees

Ye shall receive power, after that the Holy Ghost is come upon you ; and ye shall be witnesses unto me both in Jerusalem, and all Judaea, and in Samaria, and unto the uttermost part of the earth —Acts i: 8.

I WANT to talk to you on the topic, "You Can Be Adequate." We had during the war among our American casualties the loss of a chaplain, who was the son of a dear friend of mine, Dr. Daniel Poling, Editor of the American *Christian Herald.* His fine preacher son felt led to enlist in the Chaplains' Corps. Not very long after his enlistment he was sent overseas, and the ship on which he was crossing the Atlantic was torpedoed. He went down, and his body was never recovered. But there is a very lovely and gallant thing that lies back of the heroic giving of his life. It shows, I think, something of the grip he had upon his Saviour, and the grip his Saviour had on him. Just before he sailed he wrote a little note to his father and mother, and he said among other things, "Now, Dad and Mother, please don't pray simply that I shall be kept safe in my service as chaplain overseas. Pray rather that I shall always be adequate." I suggest to you that is a brave and a Christian prayer. "Don't pray that I shall be safe, necessarily, but pray that I shall be adequate"— matched, by the great grace of the Saviour, against any thing, any circumstance, any contingency, any experience, any eventuality.

Now, surely, if any group of men and women needed the under-girding of some such assurance as that which came from the lips of Jesus in our text, it was this group, gathered in old Jerusalem on the day of our Saviour's Ascension. How desperately they needed to be clothed with power, to make them adequate for all that lay ahead of them; for all the opposition they were going to face; for the fulfilling of the high calling and commission to which the Saviour had already summoned them, notably in the Great Commission. In the light of all that, here they stood, far more conscious of their inadequacy than anything else; and no one

81

knew it better than the Master. So He said to them, "Ye shall receive power, after that the Holy Ghost is come upon you: and ye shall be witnesses unto me . . ."

I want to think with you first, about *the divine Person that is here presented*—the Holy Ghost. For, beloved, there is no point in our talking about the power that is made available in the lives of needy and often defeated and frustrated Christians, unless we link that power with the Person of the Holy Spirit. I want to share with you in that connection two quotations, one from another generation in my own land, and one from this generation in your land.

A good many years ago now, before the two principal branches of American Methodism came together, when we had what was known as the Methodist Episcopal Church South, covering principally our Southern States, a conference was being held, presided over by a very godly and Spirit-filled Bishop, by the name of Wilson. One day he was addressing the clergy of this particular conference, and among other things he said to them, "My brethren . . ." now I quote him exactly as recorded, ". . . may it not be that much of our weakness and many of our failures are to be attributed to our ingenious efforts to find substitutes for the personal agency of the Holy Spirit?" What a suggestive phrase that is: "Substitutes for the personal agency of the Holy Spirit." One can think of a lot of things, it seems to me, that the modern church on both sides of the Atlantic has resorted to, when we need not have done so at all if we had been dependent upon and clothed with the power of the Holy Ghost.

The second quotation is from your own land, and is much more recent; it comes, interestingly enough, from a medical psycho-therapist, Dr. J. A. Hadfield, who says, looking at the church today, "One cannot but be struck with its powerlessness. It contains men of intellect, it produces the type of piety and devotion which one cannot but admire; but even its best friends would not claim that it inspires in the world the sense of power. What strikes one is the sense of impotence and failure." This realisation of lack of inspiration and power is the thing which I thought remarkable, coming from a professional man such as Dr. Hadfield. This lack of inspiration and power is associated with the fact that men no longer believe in the existence of the Holy Spirit in a practical way. They believe in God the Father, and they are reverent. They believe in God the Son, and try to follow in His steps; but for all practical purposes they are like that little band in Ephesus who had not so much as heard "whether there be any Holy Ghost," and lacking the inspiration of such a belief, they are weak, and they wonder why.

The personal agency of the Holy Ghost. What are the things in the New Testament that set forth the personality of the Holy Ghost? Well, I suggest for one thing, that the personality of the Spirit of God is implied in *the titles that He wears*. The general title is, the Spirit of God. If God is truly a personal God, and if we believe in the mystery of the Holy Trinity, as we Christians say we do, then we believe that the Holy Spirit has all the essential powers and capacities and dignities of divine personality.

But more narrowly, the distinctive title that Jesus gave Him. In that wonderfully tender and beautiful conference that Jesus had with His disciples just before His trial and crucifixion and resurrection, that supper-room meeting, our Lord gave a distinctive title to the Holy Spirit. In the A.V. it is translated "Comforter." It is variously rendered in our later translations, and the variety of renderings is due to the fact that the Greek term *Paraclete* is so difficult to carry over, with all the fullness of its meaning, into the English language; so sometimes it is translated "Advocate," sometimes "Strengthener," sometimes "Counsellor"—all these words are the attempt to convey the full body and message of the title which Jesus gave on His own authority to the third Person of the Trinity. But take what is probably the key passage: in John 14: 16 the Saviour says, "I will pray the Father, and He shall give you another Comforter"—another *Paraclete*, another Strengthener.

Now the Greek language is very remarkable in many ways, and one of the remarkable things about it is that it has such flexibility in its character. You have a choice of words which you do not have in our more poverty-stricken English tongue. And the word here translated "another" in the Greek refers to *another of essentially the same kind*. If I were to say, "I'm sorry, but I must leave Keswick immediately; I will send you *another* speaker to take my place," you would not necessarily look for a man with exactly the same colour of hair as mine, or as little hair as I have! Nevertheless you would look for one who in all the essentials of human personality is my equal. Now, when Jesus said, "I'm going away, and you won't see me as you see me now with your naked eyes; but there's an arrangement between the Father and me to send you *another* paraclete . . . I am the first one," Jesus is saying, "I stood by you. I stood with you. But I'm going to send you another. And He not only will be with you: He shall be in you, even the Spirit of truth, whom the world cannot receive because it seeth Him not, neither knoweth Him. But ye know Him, for He dwelleth with you and shall be in you."

Ah, let no man tell us—yet we do have some Christian scholars who astonishingly enough attempt to say it—but let no man tell us in the light of these facts that the Holy Spirit is an impersonal *somewhat.* He is a divine *Someone.* He is the third Person of the Trinity. That, I say, is implied in the titles that He wears. But not only so: His personality is involved in *the tasks to which He is committed.* Think of what, according to the Lord Jesus, and according to the inspired writers in the New Testament, the Holy Spirit within the Church, and through the Church to the world, is to do. I could refer to many passages in this connection, but within the limits of this hour let me be content to deal with just one passage in John 16: "And when He is come," said our Lord, referring to the Holy Ghost, "He will reprove"—mark that— "He will convince the world of sin . . ." and note this, that it is a personal ministry that He is engaged in, that can only be fulfilled by One who is a divine *personal* Convincer of sin, so far as the world is concerned. Now let your eye run down to v. 15: "Howbeit when He, the Spirit of truth, is come, He will guide you . . ." He will convince the world of sin. He will guide His disciples. He will guide *you.* It is a personal function.

Mrs. Rees and I were motoring some time ago in the State of Illinois. We stopped to visit some friends, and when we were ready to go I said to my friend, "I'm not quite sure that I know the best way out from here to the trunk highway." So my friend started to tell me that I should go to a certain corner, and look for a certain sign . . . and he ended up by saying what always makes me a little bit dubious; he said, "You can't miss it!" When anyone says, "You can't miss it," I'm sure to miss it! So seeing that I was a bit fearful he kindly said, "I'll hop in my car and lead you out to the trunk road." Well, I hadn't to bother about signs; all I had to do was to keep my eye on my friend. A sign is an impersonal thing. It has its value, obviously; but how much better to have a guide, a leader, and a director. That is the Holy Spirit. Said Jesus, "He shall guide you . . ."

He shows His personality by the tasks which He is committed to carry out. Says Jesus, "He shall not only convince the world; He shall not only guide you; he shall *glorify me* . . . for He shall take of mine, and shall show it unto you" (v. 14). The Holy Spirit as a Convincer, the Holy Spirit as a Director, and the Holy Spirit as a Revealer. Now these, my friends, are functions of personality. By the tasks to which He is committed, the Holy Ghost is clearly set forth as a Person.

I have but one thing more to say before I pass to the next consideration, and that is that the personality of the Holy Spirit is not only implied in the titles that He wears, and involved in the tasks to which He is committed; it is also indicated in *the treatment which He may be accorded.* Let us think of the offences which may be committed against the Holy Ghost. He may be vexed; He may be quenched; He may be blasphemed; He may be resisted; He may be grieved. Now with the possible exception of the one from Ephesians 4, "Quench not the Spirit," you have clearly indicated the personality of the Holy Spirit, because these are treatments that you could not accord to a mere *thing*, a somewhat, an impersonal force or energy. No, these are offences that you can commit only against personality.

So it is that Jesus is saying to us today, as He did so long ago to those disciples in Jerusalem, "I am presenting you with One who is God! God in you—God in you individually, and God in you collectively; God in His Church." For the Holy Spirit in this dispensation, when our Lord as to His bodily presence is in His session at the right hand of the Majesty on high—from whence, blessed be His Name, one day He is coming again—is the Administrator of the affairs of the Church, under the Lordship of Jesus Christ, the Church's Head. And if we want the churches of Britain and America in these days to be illumined and inflamed with the passion and power of the early Church, we must be driven again as Christians to recognise and magnify the personality and the deity and the dignity of the Holy Spirit.

That brings me to a second matter for consideration. I want you to think not only of the divine Person presented, but of *the divine power promised.* "Ye shall receive the power of the Holy Spirit coming upon you." Now, contrary to what I fear is the popular idea, even in Evangelical circles, may I say that this power to which the Master is referring is not primarily power for miracles and for things spectacular and sensational—the kind of service that many people regard as a touchstone of success. Now I do not say that rashly; and I should like to tarry with the point long enough for you at least to understand what I mean by it, whether you can find yourselves in total agreement or not.

Has it occurred to you—or if it has, have you really pondered it as it deserves to be pondered—that long before the day of Pentecost these men to whom Jesus was speaking had received and had demonstrated amazing power in the arena of ministry and service? You take, for example, the record in Matthew 10: 8, when our Lord sent out the twelve, and said, "With the power and authority I'm going to give you, heal the sick, cleanse the lepers, cast out devils, raise the dead: freely ye have received, freely give." I submit to you that this healing of the sick and cleansing of lepers, casting out devils and even raising the dead, is sensational power in service. And these men had that long before Pentecost, and they demonstrated it.

Take another bit of evidence. The passage just referred to has to do with the sending out of the twelve. In Luke 10 we have the narrative of the sending out of the larger company, the seventy. And Jesus filled them with power for ministry and service. They went out to exercise that power, and they had a tremendous time—so much so that they came back simply elated; they were glowing with the things they had achieved, and they said, "Why, Lord, even the devils are subject unto us!" And somehow Jesus read something there that did not kindle any great enthusiasm in His own heart, and so He said to them, interestingly enough, "That was to be expected. I gave you power to tread on scorpions and serpents; power over all the power of the enemy. Notwithstanding, in this—this sensational achievement—rejoice not, in the first instance. Don't be carried away by that, as though it were more important than anything else; but *rather, that your names are written in heaven.*"

Now I want to say a very pointed thing to you. From that day until this, it has been the tendency of carnal Christians and a carnal Church to be more interested in power for performance, than it has been interested in power for purity; more interested in power for conquest than in power for Christ-likeness. And Jesus read it as you would read your A.B.C.'s. You see, at the very start, while these men were exercising a power to cast out devils, a power to heal sick people, a power to cleanse lepers, they were still without a power working inwardly and centrally, that would make them in the depths of their souls one with their Master. So we have these contradictions in their lives. We need to stress the fact that the power of the Holy Ghost is power for Christ-likeness before ever it is power to go out and do things that produce headlines in the newspapers. It is power to be like our blessed Lord in mind and motive and spirit.

These were the contradictions. The very same men with power over diseases and demons, did not have power over their own spirits without jealous bickerings among themselves. They did not have power that dealt with the unholy ambitions that boiled up out of their hearts. James and John asking the Lord, "In the kingdom, may one of us sit on Thy right hand, and the other on the left?" Now one of the Gospel writers says that request was made by James and John: another says it was made by their mother. So the critics say, "There you are! A contradiction!" There is no contradiction at all. You see, it ran in the family, this seeking for the high place, wanting to be noticed and preferred and honoured above others. Jesus said, "Ye know not what ye ask: can ye drink of the cup that I drink of?" The law of the cross—mark it, the law of the cross now—they were not prepared for that.

A profound and a probing and a purifying power that deals with this unholy ambition. You recall that when the rest of the apostles heard about this self-assertiveness and ambition of James and John, "they were filled with indignation." They were resentful; they were censorious about it. And again, there was the case of John, the winsome and usually well-behaved John, getting terribly annoyed because the Samaritans did not give Jesus the hospitality that he thought they should; and so he said, "Lord, shall we command fire to come down out of heaven and consume them?" Jesus had to say to him, "Why, John, what kind of spirit is that?"

My brethren in the ministry, may I say to you as to my own heart, You can have power that seems to sway a multitude, power to prepare and deliver impressive sermons, power of eloquence, power to administer a parish cleverly, skilfully; but have you power in your own home, with your own wife and your own children, with your own officers in the church? Have you power to be Christlike—Christlike in your mood, Christlike in your manner, Christlike in your spirit?

Here, you see, is the evidence of the need for power for Christlikeness, that Jesus read so unerringly in the hearts of those disciples. So I press it home to your heart. Do not be concerned in the first instance about power that is going to make you a Christian worker, or a missionary or a church officer about whom people will be talking; someone who will be written up in the columns of the religious or the secular press. Oh, no! What we need is power to bring us right down into living union with the mind of our crucified and risen Saviour.

Not only is power needed for Christlikeness, but related to it there is *power for co-ordination*. That was a wonderful prayer that David once prayed—and there are some great insights, you know, in the inspired writings of the Old Testament concerning even the subjective side of experience; one can almost call it Christian experience, because its insight is so keen. David prayed, "*Unite my heart to fear Thy Name*." Unite my heart; bring me nearer organisation, nearer co-ordination; bring to an end this cleavage, this division, this conflict in my soul. Now, mind you, there is a difference between the tensions that belong to the Christian life, and from which there is no escape, and this cleavage, this division in which we are at odds with ourselves because we are at odds with the purposes of God. God wants to bring us to the place where our hearts are inwardly coherent, where we can say to Him, "This *one thing* I do . . ."

If you are a Christian living a life of divided allegiances, partly for the world and partly for Christ, you have on your hands an inner strife, an inner disorganisation that is too much for you; but if you will turn the whole bad mess over to the Holy Spirit, He will give you an inner sense of coherence, around the unifying Lordship of Jesus Christ, so that you can say, "This *one thing* I do; forgetting those things which are behind, and reaching forth unto those things which are before, I press toward the mark for the prize of the high calling of God in Christ Jesus."

That leads me to the final message that I want to share with you, concerning *the divine purpose that is proclaimed*. We have seen, first, the divine Person presented—the Holy Ghost Himself; second, the divine power promised; and now the divine purpose proclaimed.

Why does God bring His Church to Pentecost? Why does God bring the individual believer to a personal realisation of the empowerment of the Holy Spirit in his life—a realisation that in all his difficulty the Spirit of God is omnipotent; and that if we will only allow the Spirit of God to take our fully yielded personalities, He will match them against any circumstance, any difficulty, any foe that we may be called upon to face? Well, now, obviously our Lord is not concerned about bestowing the fullness of the power of the Holy Spirit upon the Church and upon individual Christians in order that they may be thought of as some superior class of Christian. God save us from that, from every vestige of spiritual pride and Pharisaism. And quite as obviously our divine Master is not interested in bestowing upon us the fullness of the power of the Holy Spirit in order that we may be *known* as successful servants of His. A lady knelt in an after-meeting in the States, a meeting for Christians, and a friend of mine asked her, "What is the burden on your heart?" She said, "I want to be known as a successful Christian worker; so I want God to fill me with His Spirit." He said, "Well, run away! He'll never do it!"

Then he patiently showed her what he meant, that she must reach the place where she died to the desire to be *known* as successful, and be willing to be known, if necessary, as a failure, so long as she glorified her Saviour. Then God would fill her with His Spirit. He knew that this would bring to her poor, paralysed discipleship an adequacy that she had not known. He knew that this would bring to her Christian life a power that she had not experienced.

So Jesus says, The purpose of all is this, that "ye shall be witnesses unto me." Ye shall *be witnesses* unto me. I want you to notice now the aspects of that witness. We are always thinking, when we use the word "witness," of something that is done with our lips. I want you to notice that it is something that is done with your life: "Ye shall *be* witnesses."

I have a very dear friend in America whom God has greatly used. More than once he seemed to me to have the same attitude toward the full salvation message as Harford Battersby had when God used him to begin the Keswick Convention. Yesterday, passing St. John's Church, I thought about him afresh, how he was invited by a friend to go to the south of England for a conference for the promotion of Christian holiness and the quickening of the spiritual life; how he went with a great deal of prejudice and fear, and one or two of the addresses he heard put him off, and he thought it exaggerated and one-sided, and at least tending in the direction of fanaticism. Then he heard Evan Hopkins give a sermon on the healing of the nobleman's son, and he pointed out the difference between a merely seeking, a questing faith, and a *resting* faith, a faith that receives. All Harford Battersby's prejudices collapsed, and he entered into the fullness of blessing; and his life was henceforward so greatly used.

Well, my friend was prejudiced, and he used all the arguments against the full salvation message. Then one day, at the annual Detroit conference of his denomination, a Spirit-filled Bishop was presiding, who was a saint, but never as long as he lived was he a "parliamentarian." And the Detroit conference of this particular denomination was known for the number of men who were great debaters and keen parliamentarians, and some of them took almost a devilish delight in getting the presiding officer into a jam. So they got into a debate in the midst of this conference, and the chair had to make a ruling, and one of these men did not like the ruling, so he lashed out at the Bishop and told him he was wrong. And my friend the young minister sat there, and he thought, "Now, my word, this man, having insulted the Bishop like this, what the Bishop will say to him will be worth hearing! He'll put him in his place!" But as he watched the Bishop there was a radiance upon his countenance, a perfect quietness of spirit; and when the man had finished his tirade the Bishop turned to the next man and said, "Brother So-and-so, what is *your* point?" My friend said, "Like an arrow it went through me. That man has something I haven't got!"

And the Bishop had not said a word. He had not preached a sermon on the Keswick message. He was *being* a witness, a witness under test, under fire. Oh, how God wants witnesses under fire! It is all very well to talk about full salvation at Keswick, but what about the witness of your life, your manner, your spirit, when you go back home, to Lancashire, or Scotland, or down into the

Southern Counties? Then you will find there will be difficulties.
"Ye shall *be* witnesses."

One aspect of being is, of course, the aspect of speaking. I
rather agree with Sam Shoemaker, of our country—a remarkable
evangelical and evangelistic episcopalian clergyman we have—
who long ago was dealt with very strongly by the Holy Spirit.
He said, "Brought up as I was in our episcopal faith, I thought
it a shocking thing to *say* anything about any experience that
you had with your Lord. That was very privately your own.
Then," he said, "the Lord showed me not only that the New
Testament is full of vocalised Christianity; and that God uses
your tongue and speaks through your lips, but I discovered that
if you simply live the Christian life and don't tell people that it is
through Christ you are living it, *you* are more likely to get the
credit for it than Jesus is."

So here it is: witness in quiet and discreet and humble ways;
the kind of witness that focuses upon the Lord Jesus, that shows
forth not how holy *you* are, but how sanctifying and satisfying *He*
is, the Lord of glory.

Does that strike a response in your heart? "Ye shall receive
power." A divine Person presented, a divine power promised,
a divine purpose proclaimed. Is there a secret? Yes, it is the
secret of reception. "Ye shall *receive power*." There is a definite
receiving, beloved. So much of the New Testament is concerned
with receptivity. It runs contrary to our Western culture: we
want to do, to achieve. Here is receptivity. And do not be
alarmed: that is not sheer quietism. It is not something un-
natural, contrary to other aspects of teaching in the New Testament. But it does mean that you reach the place where, resistance
being broken, life having come, the source of power having been
discovered, not in your resolution of will but in the released
energy of the Holy Ghost, you receive Him. By which I mean,
you allow Him to establish the absolute Lordship of Jesus Christ
over your life. "If ye then, being evil, know how to give good
gifts to your children, how much more shall your heavenly
Father give the Holy Spirit to them that ask Him?"

ENDURING TEMPTATION

J. H. LINTON, an Anglican bishop, was one of many notable clerics who gave early support to the Keswick movement.

ENDURING TEMPTATION

Rt. Rev. Bishop J. H. Linton, D.D.

Blessed (or, *happy*) *is the man that endureth temptation*—James
1: 12.

TEMPTATION is one of the inescapable facts of life. Temptation was a fact in the life of the Holy Son of God when He tabernacled with us men; it is a fact to be reckoned with in the life of every man and woman seeking to serve the Lord Jesus Christ; and, as you read the record of the temptations of our Lord Jesus Christ, if you write that down as being only allegory, then you wipe out the inspiration that leads us men on to victory. It was not only during those forty days in the wilderness that our Lord Jesus Christ suffered, being tempted. There was one occasion on which He was talking to His disciples, and He summed up His whole three years' ministry in just two words—"my temptations." He said, "Ye are they who have continued with me in my temptations," and we know that He could not there have been referring to the forty days in the wilderness, for then He went through alone. So that, at any rate, we may begin with this word of consolation for ourselves, that even the Holy One of God, even Jesus, Very God of Very God, knew what it was to go through the fires of temptation, though He went through without sin.

It is not possible for any one of us to go very far through life blind to the awful, insidious force of temptation that besets us on every hand in our Christian life; in our boyhood, in girlhood, in the full vigour of young manhood and young womanhood, the trail of temptation lies right across our lives. Am I not speaking out of my own experience? Is it not true in the life of every one of us here? There have been times in the lives of all of us when sometimes we have felt that escape seemed almost impossible. And I know this, that when you get out into the world, and perhaps more especially when you get out abroad, away from all the restraining influences of home, then the force of temptation is certainly not lessened. Perhaps once, when you were a good deal younger, you came to this convention and listened to some of those grand old saints of God who spoke to us here of sanctification and victory, and perhaps you wondered whether they knew just what you were going through in the way of temptation. But I know that one of the saintliest men that ever spoke on this platform, when he was nearing the end of his life wrote to a friend to ask for prayer, because he found that as he grew older the force of temptation was growing ever stronger and more insistent, and he felt the need for continual prayer that he might get the victory.

Now I want to make it quite clear that I am speaking specially for those who are the Lord's own people. You have come to this convention because you wanted to get victory over sin in your life; and to all such I say, Let us go back to the Gospel record of the life of our Lord Jesus Christ Himself, and we shall see there, in His experience, what you and I are proving over and over again in our own experience, that the time of greatest spiritual uplift is the time when temptation is most intense. That was so in the life of Jesus Christ, and that is so in the life of every one of us. I can only stop just to indicate such times as: (i) At our Lord's baptism, after the Spirit of God had descended upon Him; then immediately we read that He was driven of the Spirit up into the wilderness to be tempted of the devil. (ii) Again, as He faced Jerusalem for the last time, oh! which of us can realise the awful agony as He cried out to one of His own beloved disciples, who tried to dissuade Him from all that the Cross meant, and He said, "Get thee behind me, Satan!"? (iii) Then, in the Garden of Gethsemane, in that awful paroxysm of the fury of the evil one, when the sweat burst through as great drops of blood. There was our Lord Jesus Christ's experience.

Oh! I say, let us be sure of this, that we who have come up here to this convention, and are going to get, please God, a great spiritual blessing, if we crown Jesus as King in our lives, then we, too, are bound to come into conflict with the devil, and he will seek to win the victory over us. There is no use in shirking that. And when the Spirit of God comes upon us in this convention, as He truly will if we let Him, then let us be prepared, too, to be led up by the Spirit into the wilderness. We will have our testing just after this, "for the disciple is not above his Master." And as we go up to our Holy City, with all that is going to mean for us in separation, and misunderstanding, and self-crucifixion, we, too, will have our friends who will try to dissuade us from all that the Cross is going to mean in our lives. We, too, will surely have our Gethsemane. Only then let us remember that we shall also have the angels of God standing by to strengthen us. We are not so alone in our Gethsemane as we seem to imagine.

One is compelled to speak on this subject of temptation with a deep sympathy born out of hard experience. It concerns the innermost secrets of the lives of every one of us. I know that temptations do not cease when, at the foot of the Cross, you receive the Lord Jesus Christ as your personal Saviour. They do not lessen when you get out into service for Him, and give Him your whole life for whatever that is going to mean. No, temptations do not lessen then. And when you try to let the principles of Jesus Christ rule in your business life, or when you go out to work for God as a foreign missionary, Satan never relaxes his efforts. Sometimes I think his attack comes in the nature of a barrage, when he seems to rain upon us all the explosiveness of his fury, until we seem bound to be overwhelmed with it. We have experienced that—I have, and you have. Sometimes it is in the nature of sniping from some hidden place; or else it comes in the nature of poison gas, secret, silent, deadly, paralysing, vitiating the very air you breathe.

I think there is a danger sometimes least we think of the Christian life far too much in terms of some catchy hymn-tune, whereas I know, in the experience of my own life, it is a contest in which I feel I can never afford to be caught off-guard. It was not for reclining on couches of scented rose-leaves that we were bidden to take unto us "the whole armour of God." But, men and women, here is the inspiration that comes into my life, and here is the inspiration that comes ringing down from our victorious Captain Himself: that no matter how fierce, how overwhelming the forces that are arrayed against us, these are not greater than the forces that can lead us on to victory. Right into the very heat of the furnace there stands beside us One like unto the Son of God, and He says to you and to me, "Oh! brother; oh! sister; I, too, have felt the scorching flames. I know what it means; I, too, have suffered being tempted, yet without sin—I was tempted in all points like as you are." Can that be really true? Can that mean just what it says, that the Lord Jesus Christ, when He lived as a man on this earth, was really tempted in every point just as we are? Of course it means it; for this Word of God means just what it says, and all that it says, and nothing else than what it says.

So I say, blot out for ever from your mind the thought that because Jesus was God, that therefore in some mysterious way temptation did not have the same power, the same force for Him as it has for you and me. It is this that inspires us to endure when we are feeling the force of temptation: "He was in all points tempted like as we are." Often and often I have thanked God for those words, "in all points." Then it means just this: that Jesus Christ, my Saviour, when He was a boy, was tempted just as I was when I was a boy; it means that as He grew up to be a young man, those temptations that attacked me and that attack

you too, attacked Him also. But here is the glory of it for us—
He came through victorious, without sin. So to myself, and to
every other child of God, I say, Take those words for strength,
and consolation, and encouragement to your heart, these words
of power, and just hold on to them in the hour of temptation.
They are the very word of God.

It is written again, "In that He Himself hath suffered"—oh!
thanks be to God for that—"being tempted, He is able also to
succour them that are tempted." Oh! men and women, there is
a wonderful power in sympathy, even in human sympathy. It is
a tremendous power; it wins its way right into the very heart of
the one who is suffering. Sympathy means "suffering with,"
and the one who truly sympathises with another suffers along with
that other in the moment or the hour of his suffering. Sympathy is
just a stream of love flowing out from the one heart into the other
heart, and binding the two together in a bond of love and fellowship.
True sympathy can only come from one that has truly suffered.

A lady, who is now experienced in work for her Master, told
me that once in the early days of her service she was visiting a
woman who had lost her little child; she tried to sympathise
with that mother with just such loving words of sympathy as
she knew how, and that mother looked up and, through blinding
tears, said to her, "Thank you so much; but, then, you are not a
mother, and you cannot understand." Oh! how true it was, in
the depths of her grief that mother missed something; she missed
just the tone, the look, the feeling, that would come from someone
who had suffered as she had suffered. The soul that has truly
suffered goes out in sympathy; you must know, if you are really
to sympathise. Now that is human sympathy. And Jesus Christ,
our great High Priest, the Man Christ Jesus, knows what it
means to be tempted. He, too, suffered being tempted. And
because He knows to the full the power of the tempter as he seeks
to win his victory over the soul, the heart of the Eternal God
goes out in love, and in sympathy, and in fellow-suffering with
every child of God who is enduring temptation. Thank God,
Jesus is a God who is able to sympathise to the full.

But, now, He not only knows, He not only suffers with us
when we are tempted; but it says, "He is able also to *succour* them
that are tempted"—"for in all things it behoved Him to be made
like unto His brethren, that He might be a merciful and faithful
High Priest . . . for in that He Himself hath suffered being tempted,
He is able also to succour them that are tempted." That is the
crux of the whole thing for you and for me. He overcame, and
His power is available for us, if we will use it, if we also want to
overcome.

I feel I am speaking to some who have been almost as long in the Lord's service as I have been in the world. You can look back and say, "These forty years hath He led me, and there hath not failed one word of all His good promises which He hath promised," but there are others, perhaps, who have only just recently begun to follow Jesus Christ. You were realising the need of a Saviour who could save to the very uttermost in your life; you knew that you needed power if you were to live on the higher levels of life; and, perhaps, last year you came to the convention, and you heard a message of God here that just suited your need, and you trusted God for full salvation; and you went away filled with a joy and gladness that you never before had realised. All was joy—for a time; and then somehow temptation seemed to come upon you so thick and fast that you began to despair of ever getting the victory. You seemed to be more tempted than ever before. Out of your own heart there seemed to proceed a raging torrent of evil imaginations, and from around about you temptations seemed to become more intense, more fierce, more insidious than ever they were before, and you began to despair of ever experiencing the victory over sin. Yes, and then a horrible dread came over you lest, after all, Jesus Christ was not the victorious Saviour that you had been led to believe.

Now what does it all mean? I think this: first of all, it is true that you are being tempted more than ever before. I think that probably is true, for the devil will not easily part with his slave, even though the redemption money has been paid. I think also this, that before you gave your life to Christ, you were drifting; you were just going easily down the stream, and you were not conscious of the terrific force of the current that held you in its grip. Now you have begun to pull against the stream, and you are realising how strong the current is. You cannot drift against the stream. Or, if I may put it in another way, you can shut off your engine and trolley downhill with the engine off—and the steeper the hill the more swiftly you go; but it takes a good engine, well tuned, to go uphill on top, and sometimes it is conquest if you creep up at all. But perhaps this is the most encouraging fact of all, that God has allowed you to go into the wilderness to be tempted, because God knows that you are going to win through. In the war the trusted regiments were put in the place where the battle waxed hottest and the fighting was strongest; and, the very enduring of temptation is going to be a blessing—God says so. Sometimes when we are weary, the voice of the Captain comes, and He says, "But do you really want to give in? Would you really like to give up the contest, and leave the devil triumphant?" Oh! you ask the youngest soldier in the King's army! And "we wrestle not against flesh and blood, but against principalities, against powers, against spiritual wickedness in high places." God calls us to a fight in which we never lay down our arms this side of victory. "Blessed is the man that endureth temptation."

"The trial of your faith worketh patience"—worketh patience? Yes, but not that passive idea that so often we connect with the word. The word has a military ring about it; it is the idea of holding out to the end. Here is a little band of soldiers, and they are out there, in a difficult post, with the enemy all around them. Help is long in coming; the enemy call on them to yield, and those soldiers just think of that king whose flag they defend, and they know that behind them they have the whole might of his forces: so they stiffen their backs to the struggle; they dig in deeper than ever, and hold out to the end. There is patience. And "the trial of your faith worketh patience," that sort of patience.

Now, again, temptation is not sin, because the Lord Jesus was tempted. It is giving in which is sin. Oh! men and women, I want to say this now, that the Christian man or woman, with all the resources of God to draw upon, has no right to give in to the evil one. That is treachery to the Master whose name you bear. The promise of God in His Word is, "Sin shall not have dominion over you"; and where sin has had dominion over the child of God, then it just means that the child of God had not used the resources which God has meant us to use. I think sometimes, perhaps, we need to emphasise that to our own hearts even more than to preach it. The Word of God gives no authority whatever for any Christian willingly to consent to a standard of life in which sin gets the upper hand. If we do so consent, then we are deliberately betraying our Master, and we are daring to set up a standard of life lower than that which God summons us to in His Word. It just amounts to this: Here is God's own Word, that liveth and abideth for ever, and the testimony of the Word of God is this, that God calls us not to a life of defeat, but to a life of victory. And when we speak of renouncing the devil, what does it mean? It means throwing back the challenge to the tempter, and saying, "Come along, Satan; I will fight." That is renouncing the devil.

Again listen to the Word of God: "When he is tried he shall receive a crown of life." That crown is promised to the man who is tried and tested, and who triumphs. I suppose in the days of the war we should have looked doubtfully at the soldier who came out of the fray with a clean tunic, and not a splash of mud on it, and we reserve our cheers for the little drummer boy who went out into the zone of danger to rescue his officer. The Victoria Cross is not given to the man who stops at home, but to the man who dares death in the path of duty; to the man who comes, scarred, it may be, and maimed, through the battle, but triumphant. "Blessed is the man that endureth temptation."

Now I want to be practical. The vital question is this: Do we want to triumph? Do we want to have sin done with for ever in our lives, or do we want to go back occasionally to the old sins and the old haunts, back to the pleasures of sin for a season? Then let us be quite frank with ourselves about it; let us tell God what we mean to do. We may go back occasionally to the old sins and to the old haunts, and we may listen to the voice of the tempter when he says it does not matter to give in just once in a while; and God knows there are pleasures in sin—that is the fascination of it. And then we give in. Oh! but then we hear the thunder of God saying, "Know thou that for all these things God will bring thee into judgment; whatsoever a man soweth, that shall he also reap." If you sow wild oats, you cannot expect to reap good grain; if you sow to the flesh, you will reap corruption; if you sow the wind, you will reap the whirlwind.

So we come back now to the question: Do you want to win? You have come up here because you want to win, have you not? Now do you want it at any cost, at anything it may mean in self-crucifixion? Then let us ask ourselves now, Am I willing, this very hour, to make a clean cut with sin? "Willing?" you say. "God knows I am willing, but I cannot." Then I ask you, if God were to empower you now, would you be willing to face all that it means, all that a full deliverance from sin would mean in your life? Would you be willing to face the consequences of that? Then will you take God at His word, that word that never fails? Do you know these lines? I think they are A. B. Simpson's—

> There are some who believe the Bible,
> And some who believe a part;
> Some who trust with a reservation,
> And some with all the heart.
>
> But I know that its every promise
> Is firm and sure always:
> It is tried as the precious silver,
> And it means just what it says.

Will you come out on that word of God, that means just what it says? Will you plead the promises of God, and put God on His honour to fulfil them in your life?

Here is, then, the promise of victory: "There hath no temptation taken you but such as a man can bear, and God is faithful and will, with the temptation, make also a way of escape, that you may be able to bear it"—and I think that means that every temptation carries with it its own way of escape. This is the promise of victory; I have already referred to the promise of sympathy which we get in the verse: Jesus Christ "was in all points tempted like as we are, yet without sin," and, "in that He Himself hath suffered being tempted, He is able to succour them that are tempted."

Then there is the promise of reward to him that overcometh. Oh! men, it would be the most cruel mockery of God to hold out the promise of reward to the man that gets the victory if conquest was impossible. You cannot believe such a caricature of God as that. "To him that overcometh." Then thanks be to God, it means that conquest is possible. Will you take that as a pledge from God that you may attain unto this life of conquest, and then you will be able to look up with the apostle Paul, and say, "Thanks be unto God who always causes us to triumph in Christ Jesus." I ask you, will you take it? Do you want that life of victory to-night? Will you face up to the consequences? Will you take God at His word, put Him on His honour, and go out, knowing victory over sin in your life?

BUT IF NOT ...

J. STUART HOLDEN graduated from Cambridge and studied theology under Handley C. G. Moule at Ridley Hall. He became the Anglican curate at Walcot, Bath, yet devoted much of his time to itinerant evangelistic work. He delivered this address at Keswick in the summer of 1914, a few weeks before the start of World War I.

BUT IF NOT . . .

Rev. J. Stuart Holden, M.A.

I suppose it is safe to say that the majority of us have been led by the proclamation of God's truth, and in all the illumination of His Spirit in these gatherings, to expect large changes in our experience, large renewals of strength and grace, large openings of fruitful service: and with these expectations we are leaving this place of vision, to return to the valley of duty.

I want to speak as simply—and God knows I want to speak as tenderly—as may be to those who, in the days to come, may not realise these expectations; to those who in days to come, and not many days hence, are going to be sadly disappointed because their experience does not reach out to their expectation. I want that each one of us shall see that God has larger meanings in life than we are now able to read, that God has larger answers to our prayers than we are able to anticipate, that God has a thousand ways of fulfilling His promise in human lives that trust Him; that so, forewarned by this knowledge of God's wondrous greatness and transcendence, we may be forearmed against the perils of disappointment, forearmed against that disheartening of soul which makes our hearts the ground, the fruitful ground, for the most noxious seed the devil can ever sow there.

Therefore I want to speak to you on three simple words, as you find them in Daniel 3: 18. Let me read with you from verse 16, which will recall the incident, of which this is part, to your minds. "Shadrach, Meshach, and Abed-nego answered and said to the king, O Nebuchadnezzar, we are not careful to answer thee in this matter. If it be so, our God whom we serve is able to deliver us from the burning fiery furnace, and He will deliver us out of thine hand, O king. *But if not*, be it known unto thee, O king, that we will not serve thy gods, nor worship the golden image which thou hast set up."

You remember the story well. Challenged not to worship God at all, challenged to bow down to the popular idol, challenged to join the fickle multitude in acclaiming an earthly king, to the degradation of the King of their hearts, with a burning fiery furnace in front of them as an alternative to obedience, this is the answer of the three Hebrew children—"Our God is able to deliver us. More than that, our God will deliver us. More than that, if He does not deliver us, we are still not going to worship your idol. If He does not deliver us, our faith is not at an end. If He does not deliver us, our resolution is entirely unshaken: we still believe God."

Now, beloved, it may be for you and me that the experiences we have sought here, that the prayers we have offered here, the hopes that have been aroused here, are none of them going to be realised just in the way we have imagined. It may be that you who have claimed a deliverance which you have seen as part of God's plan in your life, are going to find that God works by human co-operation with His divine Spirit, and that your way of deliverance is a *Via Dolorosa*. It may be that you, my brother, who have claimed a Pentecost from God, are going to find that it leads you not to a revival, but to tremendous Satanic opposition. It may be that in your church or mission you are not going to see a great ingathering of souls at all, but a great revolt of worldly Christians and church officers. It may be that from Keswick you are going into a pathway which is dark with the mysteries of God's dealings with you. And let me say to you here, that if your faith has not got an alternative, you are going to be worsted. If you are going to be bowled over because of the things which, in some shape or form you are bound to meet, then the world which is looking on, and which is taking its measure of Jesus Christ from the loyalty and fidelity of your witness to Him, is going to be staggered. Oh, blessed be God, our gracious God, who teaches our hands to war and our fingers to fight, who is our Hope and our Fortress, our Battle-axe and our Deliverer. Blessed be God who speaks to us ere we go from this place into the unknown life of peril and danger and opposition. Let us see to it that our faith has an alternative to our present expectation. Blessed is the man who goes down from Keswick saying something akin to that which these three Hebrews said to the great king who vaunted himself against God: "We will not serve thee; we will not bow down to thine image, even if God does not do for us as we have trusted Him to do." O God, give us a faith like this!

Do not think that this is faithlessness on the part of these men. Read their protestant words: "Our God is able and He will; *but if He does not*, we still recognise His will as entirely supreme. If He does not, we still reckon God as greater than our hearts and all their imaginings. If He does not do just what we thought He was going to do, we still believe, though we have no evidence of sense to support our faith." This is the faith which accepts God's will not merely with equanimity but with positive enthusiasm. This is the faith which relates itself not only to the commands of

God, but to His contradictions; and if you and I go on with Him
we shall find that pathway to be one of constant contradiction:
Christ contradicting my conceptions; Christ my Teacher contradicting my impulse and my aims; Christ my Master bringing all
things within me into conformity with His holy purpose. Oh,
this is not faithlessness; it is faith, which says, "But if not, my
course is already clear; if not, my determination has already been
made; if not, my resolve is entirely unaltered, for it has been made
in the conscious presence of God, and on the warrant of His own
sure Word."

Beloved, it is by these contradictions oftentimes that God teaches
us in ways which otherwise were impossible either to Him or to us.
There are words which I often read to my own enlightening and
comfort, and you will allow me to repeat them to you now—

> If all my years were summer, could I know
> What my Lord means by His "made white as snow"?
> If all my days were sunny, could I say,
> "In His fair land He wipes all tears away"?
> If I were never weary, could I keep
> Close to my heart, "He gives His loved ones sleep"?
> Were no griefs mine, might I not come to deem
> The life eternal but a baseless dream?
> My winter and my tears and weariness,
> Even my griefs may be His way to bless;
> I call them ills, yet that can surely be
> Nothing but love that shows my Lord to me.

In these days which lie ahead of each one of us, with their
perplexing experiences, remember that His meanings of life are
essentially larger than ours; and it will fill our hearts with peace
and put stability into our lives to be able to say, "But if not,
Lord, I still trust Thee; and if not, I am here as truly Thine as
ever I was; as truly Thine in the darkness of London, of the
slums, of the mission field, of the unsympathetic home, as truly
Thine, my God, in the darkness as I was Thine in the light at
Keswick. But if not——!"

This alternative to disappointed faith tests the entire quality of
the man who professes the faith of God. I know the man—I have
him in mind to-night—who, being disappointed in his experience,
nervously begins to pity himself; the man to whom self-conse-
quence is everything. When God contradicts his expectation and
longing, his faith is staggered and his backsliding begins. I know
the man who is willing to accept the shallow answer to a great
question, the man to whom disappointment becomes disbelief,
the man who measures God in the tiny scales of his own self-

consciousness. Many a one such has gone from Keswick to be utterly disheartened, utterly despondent, and ultimately a deserter. He had never learned to say, "But if not, my God; but if not!"

There is a subtle interaction in the life of every one of us of courage and conscience; and the man who does not stand firm with God and for Him, who loses his integrity, loses also his power of vision, because one experience of his faith staggers him. On the other hand, I know the man who has learned to say courageously with these three Hebrews, "But if not . . . there shall be no deviation from my duty; its dominance shall be entirely unaffected in my life. But if not—if no ecstatic joy fills me, if no revival fruits appear in my work, I mean to go on and do the next thing. If I do not get the sunshine in all its full-orbed light upon my life, I mean to follow the gleam which I have already seen. If I cannot see the distant scene, I can see at least one step. God has given me enough light to walk by, and therefore, if not, I am going on with my work. If not, there shall be no cessation of hostility to evil, no begging out of the conflict with all the forces of the devil in the world. There shall be no lowering of my aim, even if I am conscious of repeated failure." The crime of our lives is not failure, but low aim; and by the grace of God, forgetting the things that are behind, I press on toward the mark for the prize. Even if the battle seems to be going against me, there shall be no desertion of the colours.

My friend there, the business man, has come to a determination to seek first the Kingdom of God in his business, that all things else may be added to him; and he finds not additions, but subtraction; he finds that his profits are not greater, but less each year. He finds that the pathway of the cross is no sentimental, emotional thing to sing about, but that the cross is heavy and the way is narrow and the positions innumerably difficult for the man who says, "But if not, I do not intend to pull the flag down; if not, I do not intend for a moment to desert my Lord, for I can never unsee what I have seen in Him, and I can never unlearn what I have learned from Him, and I can never lose that which He has begun to work in me. Therefore, be the consequences of my fidelity what they may, I am going on with God."

After all, beloved, if you have the real faith of a child as you leave Keswick, and in consequence of God's drawing near to you here, it is founded not upon a subjective experience, but upon God Himself. My faith does not stand in the wisdom of men; my faith does not stand in the memory of an emotional thrill which came through me, lifting me on to a higher life in this place; my faith does not rest upon anything that is visible, but upon that which is within the veil, where Jesus is. Therefore in the calm confidence of a child I may say with these three young Hebrews, "I am expecting God to do wonderful things for me; I am expecting God to break down iron gates before me, and to beat down my foes all around me. I am expecting God to give me great and wonderful power in His work, manifested by souls gathered in and wondrous revival all round. But if He does not, I am still going on with Him, persuaded that He doeth all things well, and that His wisdom is my sheet-anchor."

Now, beloved, let me point out to you that God's response to this spirit is to do a bigger thing than we trust Him for, not a smaller. These men said, "Our God is able to deliver us from your fire. What do we care about your old furnace, heated seven times? It does not affect us; it does not even make us perspire with fright: we are absolutely calm in front of it." But, mind you, God did a far bigger thing for them than they thought He would do. He did not deliver them from the peril at all, but He delivered them in it: and that is an infinitely greater thing. He did not effect their escape from the furnace, but He gave them an experience of fellowship in the furnace that they had never dreamed of, for Jesus Himself came to walk with them in that furnace. I wonder what they talked about! They did talk, and they heard words there which it is not lawful for men to utter or to imagine; and they learned more in that furnace with Jesus than they had ever dreamed it possible for men to know of God. That is the kind of thing God does to the men who have this spirit. They said, "He is going to check your hand, O king"—but He did not do it at all—He did something greater: He changed the king's heart, He brought the king to a knowledge of His almighty power and grace. And, beloved, great though your expectations are, they are not great enough; great though the promises are to your conception to-night, that conception is not nearly great enough. God is going to do an infinitely larger and more influential thing in our lives, if we will stand with Him.

Very briefly, let me point out to you that this is not an isolated instance. I find this principle running right through the Word of God. Let me give you an illustration or two. God said to Abraham, "Take now thy son, thine only son Isaac," and he took him, and together they mounted the hill. I hear the boy saying to the father, "Father, here is the wood for the sacrifice, but where is the lamb?" And I hear Abraham say to him, "My son, God will provide Himself a lamb; *but if not*, the programme is going to be carried out. But if not, there is going to be a sacrifice. My purpose is entirely undeterred; my obedience to God is entirely unaltered; my devotion to God is entirely unmoved, even if He does not provide a lamb, and if I have to put my son to the knife and to the fire." That is the secret of Abraham's fruitfulness—his faithfulness; that is the secret of God's blessing to the nations through that man.

I see it again in a man who has lost everything. His home is gone, his friends are against him, his health is gone. He sits there mourning, and under the mourning there is a note of triumph. "God shall bring me forth to the light, and I shall behold Him." Then he says, in effect, "*But if not*—though He slay me, yet will I trust Him. Even if He does not bring me out to the place where I behold His face in righteousness, I shall still trust Him. I know that my Redeemer liveth."

I remember another man. He is in prison—a man persuaded of Christ's identity and mission, a man who stands for the most wondrous self-effacement this world has ever seen, a man who cried to others, "Behold the Lamb of God," and rejoiced when his own disciples left him to go with Jesus; a man who knew the power of God in his life, for he was filled with the Holy Ghost from his birth; a man who saw in Jesus the great Baptizer with the Holy Ghost and with fire; and a man whose faithfulness was put to such severe test as you and I have never known, in the prison-house on the shores of the Dead Sea. He sent his disciples to Jesus—the Jesus who said He had come to liberate the prisoners, and here is one of His loyal friends whom He does not liberate. Here is the One whom he has proclaimed as the mighty Messiah of God, but He seems so slow at coming to the victorious side of His work. John sends his disciples to Jesus and he says, "Master, have I, after all, been mistaken? Art Thou He that should come? I thought you were; *but if you are not*, I am still going on to look for another, for the promises of God cannot be broken."

I think of Paul, too. Oh, those wonderful, those magnificent declarations of Paul's faith. Listen to them above the howling of the tempest. "I am persuaded that neither death, nor life, nor angels, nor principalities, nor powers, nor things present, nor things to come, nor height, nor depth, nor any other creature, shall be able to separate us from the love of God, which is in Jesus Christ our Lord." "In all these things we are more than conquerors, through Him that loved us." "Thanks be unto God, which always causeth us to ride in triumph in Christ." And he ended—where? In a prison; not in a great burst of praise and victory, but in a prison, chained to two Roman soldiers. But Paul had this "if not" spirit in him; and if you want to read its expression, turn to his prison Epistles; turn to the words that came from his heart in that prison-house in Rome, and you will see the indomitable spirit of the man who was filled with the Spirit of God.

But before I close there is Someone higher, greater than Abraham, and Job, and John, and Paul; there is the Blessed One Himself. Oh, beloved, listen for a moment. Away there yonder in the Garden He cries, "Father, if it be possible, let this cup pass from me; *but if not*, Thy will be done." That is the spirit that made the world's redemption an accomplished fact; and that is the spirit in you and me which will invest our lives with redemptive value, as we go out from the throne of God down to the gutter of sin to do the work of the Redeemer. This is the spirit, and the only spirit, which means victory beyond anything we can conceive.

So as we turn from Keswick in these few closing moments, may God make this your spirit and mine, in view of all the future may hold, in view of all the mystery that may becloud your pathway, in view of all that may stagger you for a moment as God's greater thoughts are brought into conflict with your own inferior and unworthier thoughts concerning His purpose. When your prayers, instead of being speedily answered, are delayed of answer; when those things you thought God must do for you He still keeps you waiting for, O God help each one of us to say in some such words as these, "But if not"—

> I'll follow Thee, of life the Giver;
> I'll follow Thee, loving Redeemer;
> I'll follow Thee, deny Thee never;
> By Thy grace, I'll follow Thee.

I will say just one thing more, and it is this: that the world is perfectly helpless before that kind of Christian; the world is perfectly helpless before the man who positively laughs at its shams, because he knows what they are worth. The world is perfectly helpless before the man who goes into the fire for God with a song in his heart. It cannot light a fire, however vehement its flame, that can do more than burn up a man's bonds and bring him into greater liberty.

> Across the path of night leads on the path of God;
> Not where the flesh delighteth, the feet of Jesus trod:
> What though the path be lonely, and dark, and bleak,
> and lone,
> Though crags and tangles cross it—
> Praise God, we will go on!

That is the spirit in which to leave Keswick. And as the world is helpless before a man of that kind of faith, God cannot be otherwise than truly faithful to such a one. Therefore, as in a few minutes we shall go out into the night, and will never all meet again until Jesus comes back again, beloved, would it not be a blessing to us to bring our Keswick week to a close by solemnly, gladly re-affirming this same glad note in the presence of God to-night: "O God, I am expecting so much from Thee. Correct all my misconceptions. I am expecting Thee to do such wonderful things. My God, I am expecting Thee to make all things new with one word of Thy power. But if not: if Thou keepest me waiting, if Thou dost discipline me into patience, I here and now covenant with Thee, my Lord, that I will stand by Thee. I here and now covenant, my Lord, in all the nakedness and sincerity of my soul, that I am Thine utterly, absolutely, to the last crust and candle-flicker of life. I am Thine, Lord Jesus, for time and eternity." O God, bring us there to-night!

WHEN JESUS
IS ENTHRONED

ALAN REDPATH, a noted British Baptist who became pastor of Moody Memorial Church in Chicago, established the Mid-America Keswick Convention in that city in the mid-1950s.

WHEN JESUS IS ENTHRONED

Rev. Dr. Alan Redpath

THE second book of Samuel, chapter 5, records for us some of the events which took place in David's life immediately following his coronation day; and in Old Testament picture form it records exactly the same events which take place in the life of a child of God when the Lord Jesus Christ has a coronation day in our hearts. I trust that the Lord has stepped into His rightful place in your lives, and that He is undisputed King. Maybe only last evening in this tent He entered upon the throne of your heart, and you were able for the first time in your life to say, "It is no longer I, but Christ." Oh, blessed, happy day, when the Lord Jesus takes His rightful place, and is undisputed Lord. This is the only gateway into life; the only gateway into blessing. It is the only step into the fullness that is ours in Jesus Christ. Does Keswick teach, "Let go, and let God"? No, it does not, because the New Testament does not teach that—at least, that is only part of the truth; for the act of submission in totality to the sovereignty of Jesus Christ is but the beginning of a new régime in your heart. No longer is the puppet king self upon the throne, but the great King of kings and Lord of lords has stepped in to take the throne. If that revolutionary change takes place in a man's life, surely then there ought to be some evidence of it. There certainly is; and I wish to consider with you, *what happens when Jesus is King*.

Looking at our text for a moment: What happened when David was King? In the first place, *The sovereignty of David was immediately confirmed*; and it was confirmed in two ways. If you look for a moment at v. 7, you will see that David "took the stronghold of Zion." I am sure that most of you know the history of the people of God in the land of Canaan well enough to remember that the city of Jerusalem was always a thorn in the flesh. In spite of the fact that the whole land had been given to them, they were never, until David was king, able to possess it all; and the most strategic city, from which God's appointed king was to reign, was, alas, a city in which the enemy was deeply entrenched. The Jebusites were too much for the children of Israel, and they

113

could not cast them out (Joshua 15: 63); and then we discover
that the Benjaminites had settled down in Jerusalem on the basis
of a peaceful co-existence with the enemy (Judges 1: 8, 21).
This could not possibly be allowed to continue, so when David
became king of all Israel, we are told that he took the stronghold
of Zion. That which had baffled them through their whole
history became amazingly easy when David was king; and one
of the first evidences of the enthronement of Jesus Christ in our
lives will be that deeply entrenched habits of evil will be put
under subjection, and under the feet of our risen Lord inhabiting
the temple of the Holy Spirit—our body and mind. That which
has defied our best efforts, that which has caused us many a
heartache and many a tear, many a sense of remorse and defeat
and frustration; and that which has almost made us give up the
fight altogether—how wonderful, when Jesus is King it is put
under His feet. He comes into our lives to establish His Kingdom, and to celebrate it by giving us the first taste of deliverance
and victory over the power of inbred sin.

Have you ever noticed in your New Testament how the Lord
Jesus likes to deal with long-standing complaints? How many
instances there are of men and women who for years had been
bound by infirmity and sin, and were crippled and helpless and
hopeless, until the risen Lord came. Just one instance: that is all
we have time to recollect. When Peter and John came to the
temple to worship, and found at the gate of the Temple a man
who had been lame from his birth, Peter looked at him and said,
"Silver and gold have I none"—the Church boasted in its
bankruptcy in those days—"but such as I have give I thee: in
the name of Jesus Christ of Nazareth, rise up and walk." And
immediately the man leaped to his feet, delivered in the power
of the risen Christ.

I want to say to you in the name of the Lord Jesus, There is
no habit that has gone so deep but that the power of the blood
of Jesus can go deeper; and there is no entrenchment of sin that
has gone so far but the power of the risen Lord, by His Holy
Spirit, can go further. The first mark of the sovereignty of Christ
in a life is that the habits of years, which have baffled all our
struggles, and have brought us in shame and confession of failure
time and time again to the Lord in contrition and repentance,
the power of them is broken when He is upon the throne.

Furthermore, the sovereignty of David was not only confirmed
in this way, but it was also confirmed in that "David went going
and growing" (v. 10, margin). In other words, the sovereignty
of David was confirmed in ever increasing areas of the kingdom.
And what was true in David's life, is true in the life of the Christian.

Jesus Christ upon the throne, is but the initial step to a lifetime in which you will discover that His sovereignty is ever growing and ever extending: an ever more pleasant experience. You remember that when the angel announced to the Virgin Mary the birth of our blessed Lord, he said to her, "The Lord God shall give unto Him the throne of His father David: and He shall reign over the house of Jacob for ever; and of His Kingdom there shall be no end." And what is true prophetically, my dear friend, is true experimentally: of the kingdom of Jesus Christ in your life there is no end. It is impossible to be a Christian unless Jesus Christ is your Lord. "If thou shalt confess with thy mouth Jesus as Lord, and believe in thine heart that God has raised Him from the dead, thou shalt be saved" (Rom. 10: 9, R.V.). You cannot be a Christian unless He is crowned as Lord in your life; but the initial coronation day of the Lord Jesus is immediately followed by a succession of increasing and expanding coronations, when He becomes Lord over an ever-increasing area of your personality.

I would bear humble testimony to the fact when the Lord Jesus came into my life, at that moment, up to the limit of my understanding, He was Lord of all I had and all I possessed. But I did not know then what would be involved in surrender to His sovereignty. How thankful I am that I did not! I do not always like the sovereignty of Jesus Christ. Often, alas, I have disputed it; and every time I have disputed it, that act of resistance to His sovereignty has been followed by weeks and months of spiritual stagnation and failure when, though I did not lose my relationship with my wonderful Lord, I lost something almost as wonderful— the sense of His presence and the reality of His fellowship; and I lived for weeks and months, alas, sometimes even for over a year, in darkness, because I had again raised myself and said "No" at one point to the sovereignty of my Lord. At any point in life you can resist His sovereignty; and at that moment God puts you on the shelf: you are useless to Him. Oh, you can carry on preaching sermons, teaching a Sunday-school class, using the same shibboleths and singing the same hymns; but the unction has gone, and the uplift has gone, and the liberty of the Holy Ghost has gone, the reality has gone. The Lord is in your heart, but you have quenched His Spirit.

But I would also bear testimony to this, that every step in my life of faith and obedience has immediately been marked by a new demand made by my sovereign Lord, for His sovereignty to be displayed in another area of my life. A mark of the sovereignty of Christ in a man's life is that deeply entrenched habits are overthrown at last, and there is freedom, glorious freedom; and another mark of His sovereignty is that every step of faith and obedience is followed by the increasing demands of our risen Christ, that He may occupy a new area of your personality.

Do you find yourself putting the label "sin" somewhere in your life tonight, where you did not put it five years ago? Do you find the Holy Spirit gently but firmly and lovingly putting His finger upon something today, and saying, "You have been a Christian too long to have that. That's got to stop"? You may not have thought about it five years ago; but as you have sought to go on and grow up, the Lord Jesus has lovingly and gently and firmly led you on to an increasing experience of His sovereignty; and "of His kingdom there is no end." His sovereignty is confirmed. Is it being confirmed in your heart?

Is there someone here who, in the last twenty-four hours has had the first taste of deliverance from sin? If there is, I can tell you, you can hardly sit quiet! You are just longing to stand up and say, "Hallelujah!" You are rejoicing in liberty, freedom, under the sovereignty of the Saviour. Are you finding there is an increasing, expanding experience? Praise the Lord! You are in apostolic succession.

May I say a second thing: *The sovereignty of David was not only confirmed, but it was immediately challenged.* Notice that the Philistines gathered themselves together, and they all came up to attack him; and they spread themselves in the valley of Rephaim (vv. 17, 22). They had not been unduly concerned as long as David was satisfied to be king over Judaea; but now he was king over the whole kingdom, and this concerned the enemy greatly, and so they set up an immediate counter-attack. And they persisted in it. And may I say that immediately Jesus Christ is Lord, your act of submission is followed by a massive counter-attack from the powers of darkness. And will you notice how *pointed* was this attack. "They spread themselves." Is not that typical of the devil? How I hate him: he spreads himself all over the place! And they spread themselves in the valley of Rephaim. Where is that? That surrounds Jerusalem. Ah, Christian, will you mark this very carefully. They spread themselves upon a focal point where for years they had been tenants, although they had no business to be tenants. They had been in occupation, and had defied all the attempts of the people of God to throw them out. But once they had been thrown out, there was an immediate counter-attack to get back into occupation.

I want to be careful not to be misunderstood on this point: but I do not think it concerns the enemy unduly when a Christian signs a doctrinal statement to join a church, in which he says, "I no longer smoke, I no longer drink, I no longer play cards, and I no longer gamble." Oh, do not misunderstand me, I do

not advocate any of these things, and think it would be a great
pity if you do them: but the definition of worldliness and sin
which enables a man to say, "Because I do not do these things,
therefore I am now a consecrated Christian," is so utterly and
completely superficial. When a child of God begins to understand the meaning of the words of the Lord Jesus when He said,
"It is not from without, but from within, that there come forth
blasphemy and adultery and fornication and uncleanness and
deceit and lasciviousness and lying words," and when a man really
gets concerned about the state of his own heart, and begins to
cry with the language of Charles Wesley—

> Oh, that in me the sacred fire
> Might now begin to glow;
> Burn up the dross of base desire,
> And make the mountain flow . . .
>
> Thou who at Pentecost didst fall,
> Do Thou my sins consume:
> Come, Holy Ghost, on Thee I call:
> Spirit of burning, come.

. . . when a man gets desperate, and he cannot go on as he has
been living, and he cries out to God with all the hunger of his
soul, "Lord Jesus, set me free; cleanse my heart from secret
sin," at that point the devil launches everything he has.

Satan counter-attacks pointedly, and he counter-attacks
persistently. He will never admit defeat; and, my friend, if you
have crowned Jesus Christ as Lord, you are in for a life of constant battle and warfare. The devil did not have to bother much
about you before; but if you are concerned never to agree with
a peaceful co-existence with the enemy on any point in your
life; if you are concerned that the Lord might create in you a
clean heart, and renew a right spirit within you; might give you a
blessed experience of deliverance by the power of the indwelling
Christ, then I say to you that such light is a menace to the powers
of darkness.

The Church desperately needs in this twentieth century men
who have so submitted to the Lord that they have a testimony
of deliverance from sin. The sovereignty of Christ is counter-
attacked at every point, persistently and relentlessly. But one
other word: *The sovereignty of Christ is communicated.* What am I
to do in the midst of the battle? How am I to face an enemy
who is too powerful for me? How am I to deal with him in all
his besetting temptations upon my life? Now may I just say a
word that will help somebody? I hope you understand that

temptation is not sin. The Lord Jesus was tempted in every point as we are, yet without sin. And may I go a step further in definition, and say that sinful thoughts are not sin, either? Have you ever heard people say in conversation, "The other day this thought passed through my mind . . ." That is wonderful, just let it pass right through! Satan has no other way for attacking, except by eye-gate, and ear-gate, and thought and mind; and as he flings his poison into the heart of a child of God—and he will do it consistently and continuously and persistently—what am I to do about that?

Let me tell you this with such a glow and thrill in my soul: the sovereignty of Jesus Christ is communicated. How? Look at the story again. It was communicated in the first place *by prayer*: "David enquired of the Lord" (vv. 19, 23). On both occasions when this chapter gives us the record of an attack of the enemy, it goes on to say that David got straight on his knees, and said, "Now, Lord, it's up to you." My friend, it is just as well he did so on both occasions, for do you notice that the divine strategy for victory in the first instance was totally different from the strategy in the next? In the first instance it was go and attack; in the second instance it was sit still and wait. If David had followed the strategy of yesterday in the battle of today, he would have missed all divine resources, and he would have been humiliated in defeat.

What do I do in the face of the enemy who attacks when Jesus Christ is the Lord? I get on my knees: or if I am not in a place where I can do that, I lift up my heart and say, "Now, Lord, it's up to You. I have no might and I have no power, and I know not what to do; but my eyes are upon Thee." I look up to Him, and in that moment I discover that the victory of yesterday has not put into me any strength for today. I discover, as I go on in life, that the flesh is totally corrupt. I discover that the flesh profiteth nothing, and I begin to understand the language of the apostle Paul who said, "In me, that is in my flesh, dwelleth no good thing." That is not the language of a backslider; that is the language of a man illuminated by the Holy Spirit, who has discovered that God expects nothing from him but total failure, and he can never be any different. I have been along the road thirty years as a Christian now, and every experience of the grace of God and the cleansing power of the blood of Jesus, has only made me understand more deeply than before the corruption of my own heart. Basically Alan Redpath is no different from what he was when he was saved, probably a lot worse by nature, potentially so. But I know this, that the battle is not mine, but is God's; and therefore every moment of every time of testing, first,

He communicates power through prayer. "Watch and pray, lest you enter into temptation." You will always be faced with it; but there is no need to run your head into it. Watch and pray. Enquire of the Lord, for His sovereignty will be communicated; and always listen to His communications in answer to prayer. Sometimes it is communicated by the word that says, "Go out and attack," but more often it is communicated by the word that says, "Wait for the sound of a going in the tops of the mulberry trees."

What is that "sound of a going"? Surely it is what happened when a hundred and twenty disciples in an upper room had waited and prayed for ten days; then suddenly there was the sound as of a rushing, mighty wind, and God, by the Holy Spirit, came down upon them and empowered them, and sent them out to blaze a trail for Him. That is how God communicates to my poor and needy heart constantly, His sovereignty. He communicates that sovereignty in the Person and in the power of His Holy Spirit, in answer to the man who has acknowledged his bankruptcy and submitted to the Lord's sovereignty, and who waits upon Him for the outpouring of His Spirit.

But let me say this: We do not move away from the Lord Jesus to the Holy Spirit. Oh no! He said to His disciples, "The Spirit of truth shall come to you. He shall dwell in you. I will come to you. I am in my Father, and He in me, and I in you." And the sovereignty of Jesus Christ is communicated to the poor, beaten, bankrupt, defeated heart, and yet the heart that has turned in simplicity and utter sincerity to the Lord. That sovereignty is communicated by the imparting of the life of the risen, victorious Christ into my heart and into my soul. I do not go on away from Christ to the Holy Ghost. The Holy Spirit points in my heart upward to the throne, and from that throne there is communicated the victorious resurrection life of our precious Saviour.

Oh, my beloved friends, let me say this to you: That you are no match for the counter-attacks of the enemy. I have been on the road long enough to know that the devil is far too clever and far too powerful for me. But, Hallelujah! the devil is no match for my Lord Jesus. He is no match for the Holy Spirit. And in my heart today, and in your heart if there is submission to Christ, there is throned life, sovereign life. The life of the throne in heaven has been sent back to you, to enable you to live victoriously. All the enabling that you will ever need, in every situation, is in the power of God the Holy Spirit.

As I close, listen, is there a sound of a going? Oh, has there been a sound of a going this week? Has the Spirit of conviction been abroad? You have trembled under the sound of the Word, under the sense of conviction of your failure and defeat. Has the message of sin just broken and penetrated and battered into your soul, until you have trembled under it? Has there been that deep sense of conviction; and has there been the indication that there is a balm in Gilead, and you have begun to see the answer that you need in the Holy Spirit? Is He moving upon you in conviction? Has this message been something more than theory to you: has it been life, has it been victory, has it been power?

Then listen! What does the Bible say? Bestir yourself! When thou hearest the sound of a going, bestir yourself. What are you going to do about the tremendous potential of the life of victory? Are you going to discard it because you do not understand it, or are you going to bestir yourself and act, and obey? Oh, that Jesus may fill now every heart that full surrender knows, that through that heart there may come the life-giving river, the power of a risen Christ in His Holy Spirit.